"I'm a big believer in books that don't just tell you how to do it, but actually HOW you. *In Selling Above and Below the Line*, Skip Miller shows you how to increase your sales."
—**WARREN GRESHES, author of *The Best Damn Sales Book Ever***

"Skip Miller is one of the greatest sales leaders of our time. Most sales professionals fail to sell to the fiscal buyer until the end of the month or end of the quarter. In this extraordinary book, Skip exposes the secrets to sell above and below the line to drive more revenue!"
—**CHAD BURMEISTER, VP Sales & Marketing, ConnectandSell**

"*Selling Above and Below the Line* has changed the way we sell. We are now more focused, disqualify better, and have better conversations with senior management."
—**GREG BROWN, Chief Revenue Officer, Achievers**

"Every time I encounter a Skip Miller client, they say the same thing—his stuff is powerful, simple, and my sales team actually uses it to get better. This book on changing the language you use at the C-suite is the chance for everyone else to be let in on this secret."
—**STEVE RICHARD, Founder, Vorsight and VorsightBP**

"Skip Miller and his book changed how our company sells. We now know why, when, and how to get the C-level involved in the buying process. This cuts cycle time and increases average sales price. It's the missing link between what our organization THOUGHT we knew about sales and what we really knew. There's a fine line between success and failure in sales; Skip's system is helping us stay on the good side of that line."
—**RICK ROCKELLI, Chief Revenue Officer, CQ Roll Call**

"*Selling Above and Below the Line* helped us identify the key line within our sales process that led to increased sales productivity, market differentiation, and top-line growth."
—**GREG NELSON, Senior Vice President, Global Sales, Masergy**

"Skip Miller's new book gives us the tools, knowledge, and the vocabulary to help our sales executive succeed in speaking to the C-suite."
—**RICH ELDH, Co-Founder & Managing Director, SiriusDecisions**

"The Rosetta Stone for sales teams. Brilliant!"
—**MIKE HEYLMUN, Vice President, Sales, Cosentino USA**

"By using Skip's methodology that you will find in this book, we were able to elevate the sophistication of our sales process. Our reps were finally able to effectively call into the C-suite. Our teams adopted these tools that enabled us to call higher more often. We were more prepared for sales calls, and our close rates and average sales price increased beyond our expectations."
—SCOTT WHITE, Vice President, Sales, Rackspace

"Skip Miller's new book explores a very difficult area for salespeople—getting the financial buyer engaged in the process! For those of us who are good at selling to the technical or business buyer, but find deals get stuck on the financial side, this is powerful stuff. For the legions that have implemented Skip's techniques for years, this is a new area to explore and Skip offers his typical no-nonsense way of solving those challenges."
—MICHAEL HUGHES, Senior Vice President, Worldwide Sales, Barracuda Networks

"Skip delivers one of the Holy Grails of successful selling—real tools to enable sales reps to call on higher levels in an organization—with outstanding results!"
—BRAD THORPE, Senior Vice President, Worldwide Sales, IDC

"At first glance, it may appear that, in selling to small businesses, this content isn't relevant—it very much is. *Selling Above and Below the Line* matters even when selling to a single person, the business owner. Both interests will be represented in every sale."
—AARON STEAD, Senior Vice President, Sales, Infusionsoft

"This book belongs in the hands of all associates in a company. The secret is out. The associates make the sale! Now make all of them better at it. Selling is no longer just for salespeople."
—JACK STACK, President & CEO, SRC Holdings Corporation; and co-author of *The Great Game of Business*

"Skip has a gift of making the complex very simple. By qualifying early in the process, my salespeople's productivity has shot through the roof."
—DAN THOMPSON, Sales Director North America, Trane/Ingersoll Rand

"*Selling Above and Below the Line* is simply the best at getting salespeople and managers to focus on both value propositions. These tools have made all the difference here."
—NATE VOGEL, Director, Global Sales Readiness, Tableau Software

SELLING ABOVE AND BELOW THE LINE

Convince the C-Suite.
Win Over Management.
Secure the Sale.

WILLIAM "SKIP" MILLER

AMACOM

American Management Association

New York • Atlanta • Brussels • Chicago • Mexico City • San Francisco
Shanghai • Tokyo • Toronto • Washington, D. C.

Bulk discounts available. For details visit:
www.amacombooks.org/go/specialsales
Or contact special sales:
Phone: 800-250-5308
Email: specialsls@amanet.org
View all the AMACOM titles at: www.amacombooks.org
American Management Association: www.amanet.org

This publication is designed to provide accurate and authoritative information in regard to the subject matter covered. It is sold with the understanding that the publisher is not engaged in rendering legal, accounting, or other professional service. If legal advice or other expert assistance is required, the services of a competent professional person should be sought.

Library of Congress Cataloging-in-Publication Data
Miller, William, 1955-
    Selling above and below the line: convince the C-suite: win over management: secure the sale / William "Skip" Miller. — First Edition.
        pages cm
    Includes bibliographical references and index.
    ISBN 978-0-8144-3483-3 (pbk.) — ISBN 0-8144-3483-5 (pbk.) — ISBN 978-0-8144-3484-0 (ebook) — ISBN 0-8144-3484-3 (ebook) 1. Selling. I. Title.
    HF5438.25.M56797 2015
    658.85—dc23   2014031977

About AMA
American Management Association (www.amanet.org) is a world leader in talent development, advancing the skills of individuals to drive business success. Our mission is to support the goals of individuals and organizations through a complete range of products and services, including classroom and virtual seminars, webcasts, webinars, podcasts, conferences, corporate and government solutions, business books, and research. AMA's approach to improving performance combines experiential learning—learning through doing—with opportunities for ongoing professional growth at every step of one's career journey.

Printing number
10 9 8 7 6 5 4 3 2 1

Contents

Foreword   ix

Author's Preface   xiii

Acknowledgments   xvii

1   You Are Selling More Than Just Features and Benefits *1*

The Neuroscience of Selling: It's All About Us   2

The Deceptive Lure of Features and Benefits   3

Buyers Buy Outcomes   6

2   The Line That Splits the Two Parts of a Sale *11*

Business Acumen: Knowing What Makes a Company Tick   12

Understand a Company's Network of Concerns   14

Target Two Outcomes for a Sales Process That Works   15

The Split: Selling Above and Below the Line   18

Uncover the Buyer's Multiple Personalities   20

Focus on Two Value Propositions   22

3   Selling Below the Line *23*

The Rationale for Features and Benefits   24

Two Sales Processes, Two Results   28

WIIFM: The Five Ps   31

The BTL Buyer's Mantra: I Need It and I Like It   33

The Three Levels of a Purchase   34

Company Win and Personal Win   35

4   *Know Your ATL Buyer* *36*

Change: We All Face It, and We All Fear It   37

The Fear Factor   39

Promote the Positive Motivators   41

Time Zones: Great Salespeople Are Time-Travelers   44

5   *Understanding ATL Energy* *49*

Capturing the Energy of a Sale   49

Harness the Energy in ATL Events   54

Other ATL Oddities   58

Change Is King   60

6   *Controlling the Inbound Sale* *61*

Inbound Qualifying Made Easy   62

Lead Scoring   62

Find the Need with the Three Levels of Why   63

Qualify and Disqualify   67

Getting Control, Starting with the Welcome   68

7   *Controlling the Outbound Sale*..............................*73*

Make Outbound Qualifying Work for You   73

Your Homework   75

Getting Past the Screen   77

Get to the Point—The One That's All About Them   78

The Prospect's Homework   79

Gives/Gets   80

8   *Stage 1: Being ProActive* *82*

Prospecting to the ATL Level: Strategy and Tactics   82

Mastering the Art of the Short Email   85

How to Leave a Phone Message   89

Trumpeting   93

9   *Basics Never Go Out of Style* *95*

Start the ATL Phone Call with a 30-Second Speech   95

The Art of Asking Questions   100

Paraphrasing and Summarizing Skills   104

Time-Traveling   105

Next Step   106

10   *Sharpen Your Executive Business Acumen* *108*

Top Down and Bottom Up   108

Think Across the Entire Organization   111

ATL and BTL Solution Boxes   114

Talking About Trains   115

Become the Champion of Solution Box B   117

I-Date for Box B   118

11   *Stage 2: Don't Forget The Split* *120*

It's Not a Race   123

The Quantified Problem   124

The Quantified Cause   129

The Quantified Solution   130

Printer Story: The Value of the Three Qs   130

12   *Discussions with an ATL Executive* *136*

The ValueStar: Learning ATL Vocabulary   136

ROI: Selling Money   137

Making the Most of Time   140

Risk: The Million-Dollar Question   142

Leverage: Building Value Across Trains   146

Brand/Image: The Emotional Value   148

13   *Creating and Controlling ATL Energy* *150*

The Golden Rule   152

The Salesperson's Energy   152

14   *The "How" of Controlling the ATL Sale* 161
ATL Energy: Finding Additional Trains   161
BTL Energy   170

15   *Stage 3: Value vs. Value* 175
Two Value Conditions   176
A Day in the Life . . .   180
BTL and ATL "I Get It" to "I Get It"   183
Validation vs. Education   184

16   *Balancing Between the Lines to Accelerate the Deal* 188
Energy Sources   188
Moving the Chains ATL   191
Learn to Quantify Energy   192
Getting to Quantification with Impact Analysis   195
Solution Boxes and I-Dates   198

17   *Stages 4 and 5: Getting a Decision* 200
The Goal Is a Decision   200
The Power of Options   204
Getting a Decision—Now   205

18   *How to Implement ATL/BTL Selling in Your Current
Process* 210
Map Your Stages   210
Visual Collaboration with the Customer   212
Next-Step Selling   214

19   *Overall Strategizing for an Above the Line Sale* 220
Managing Risk by Relying on Numbers   221
Know Your Options   223
Wine Ages Well. Problems Don't.   226
Look at All the Options   226
Final Thoughts   227

Index 229

Foreword

Sales. That's your profession, right? Isn't this why you picked up this book?

Sure, you've read sales books before. They typically teach selling tactics, pipeline stages, and sales tricks. They teach salespeople how to pitch. Problem is, that only goes so far. Why? Because fundamentally, who wants to be sold? Truth is—nobody. But, everybody wants to buy!

In this book, Skip Miller will teach you how to help people buy. That's what good salespeople do. We ask the right questions. We listen. We help our customers identify and solve their problems. We speak their language. What we really do is help them buy. Skip outlines simple tools that will help you help people buy.

How do I know this? Skip was our first sales trainer at Tableau. He has been a key partner as I have led our sales team at one of the fastest growing software companies in the world. During the four years that Skip has trained us, our sales team of seventy has grown over ten-fold. Over the same period, Tableau's annual revenue growth grew over 80 percent! Yes, that fast.

At Tableau my leadership philosophy is all about busting through belief barriers. When most people talk about getting better at sales, they talk about the mechanics, but I've learned through my own experience in sales—from selling educational books door to door during college to building one of the most successful sales teams in technology at Tableau—that *belief* is the most powerful sales tool in the world. At Tableau, our reps *believe* in our mission: "To Help People See and Understand Data." We believe in our product. We believe we can help virtually anyone. And Skip has been a fundamental contributor in helping me build *belief* on the Tableau sales team.

I knew this from the start when I began using Skip's sales tools after reading his first book, *ProActive Selling*. I remember one of our first interactions when we were negotiating his initial Tableau training contract. I started using his own sales tools on him, while he was using his tools on me. This was a tough negotiation. He commented how Tableau must have a good trainer! That's Skip for you—always making a joke.

After four years, Skip is still a regular at our Tableau headquarters. He does sales training in every boot camp for new salespeople. He attends our Sales Kick-Offs. He joins our happy hours. Our team loves Skip! And here's why. Everyone learns in his training—whether a seasoned twenty-year enterprise sales professional or a brand new rep. Skip's training is fun. It's easy to understand. And, most important, it works.

OK, you are probably thinking, WIIFM? ("What's in it for me?" as Skip would say.) Good question.

In this book, Skip will teach you how to help your prospects buy. He explains how customers speak different languages. The User Buyer loves the language of features and functions. The Executive Buyer speaks the language of revenue, costs, and growth. As a salesperson, you must know how to speak both languages. Skip teaches both languages in the following pages.

Selling Above and Below the Line is full of effective sales applications. One of my favorites: Trains. Each problem is a Train. The executive buyer cares about big strategic Trains that lead to increased profits, efficiency, and market share. The more trains your solution impacts, the bigger your sale will be.

Skip ends his book with a simple theory, "Wine Ages Well. Problems Don't." So true. When it comes to wine aging well, hmm, I'll have to see. Last year, Skip gave me my very own bottle of his homemade wine. The bottle is so cool with its custom Tableau label that I have yet to pop it open. I'll eventually have to uncork it to see if Skip's wine ages well. Regarding problems though, Skip is right. Problems don't age well. When selling both above and below the line, you will need to help your customers solve problems fast. Solve their problems, and they will buy.

This book contains plenty of practical nuggets to help you become a better salesperson. And, yes, you still get the same Skip. Even the printer story that makes its way into each book. If you know what I'm talking about, you surely have a big grin on your face as you wait to turn the page to see how Skip spins the story this time.

New readers, you are also in for a treat. So get ready to learn how to help your customers buy bigger and faster. Fasten your seatbelt and enjoy the ride!

—Kelly Breslin Wright
Executive Vice President, Sales
Tableau Software

Author's Preface

"How could I have missed it?"

As a sales professional, have you ever spoken these words after a phone call or a meeting with a prospect that hasn't gone well? The usual next step is the customer telling you they are going with another solution or going in another direction. Not good.

More salespeople and sales organizations are trying to increase their average sales prices (ASP) and shorten their sales cycles. To do this, they need to call on the executive suite more often. The question is: How have you and your company prepared the sales organization to call on the executive suite?

Sales typically uses PowerPoint slides and white papers that Marketing has meticulously prepared and made everyone memorize. These expertly executed materials are all about what we do, who we do it for, and how we can do it for you, Mr. or Ms. Prospect. They work well for the features and benefits buyers (aka User Buyers), but what about the Executive Buyers? Do you really think they want to see the same story and listen to the pitch you made to the User Buyer?

For the past twenty years, we have been training salespeople and sales organizations to speak a different language when they call on the executive suite. C-levels speak a different language than their User Buyer counterparts, and it's amazing how unprepared a sales team can be to call on executives. I would guess that salespeople, on average, converse in User Buyer language in about 80 percent of sales calls they make to the executive suite. When they do get to the C-level buyer, the sales team usually asks the C-suite buyer "key" questions like:

"What would you like to know about us?"

"Here is an executive overview of what we have been talking to your subordinates about."

"What can we do so that you will approve and sign off on our deal?"

Then there are the 20 percent of sales calls that talk to the C-suite about what they want to hear—how the proposed solution can benefit one of their key goals or objectives.

"This can contribute to lowering your costs up to 20 percent."

"Timing is key to your new product launch, and this solution can help you save three to four weeks of time."

"Our solution has the potential of lowering the risk of this project by 5 to 10 points."

What's the difference between the two conversations?

TWO DIFFERENT VALUE PROPOSITIONS

There are two different value propositions in most sales. The executive suite has one idea of what they want and why they need to change what they are doing today, and the User Buyer is looking for something else. So what happens?

Salespeople go for the low-hanging fruit—the User Buyer value proposition—since that is one they have been taught how to sell to and have had success selling. And, quite frankly, they feel comfortable discussing their favorite subject, themselves.

A far sounder approach is to sell both above and below the line—to the User Buyer and to the executive suite. Early in the sales process, a focus on both value propositions substantiates your proposal's value for both levels of the organization, speeds up the sales cycle, and increases your ASP.

THE SUNDAY DINNER

Many families have a formal dinner every so often, perhaps on Sundays. When the extended family members and a few friends gather, the kids sit at one table and the adults at another. The kids' table has their own "language," and the adult table has theirs.

The kids didn't want to sit at the adult table, where they soon get bored with parent talk. Adults don't want to sit at the kids' table; they've spent plenty of time with the kids all week and long for some adult conversation.

Above-the-line (ATL) executives and below-the-line (BTL) buyers sit at different tables, talk about different things, and operate from different perspectives. Here's what is going on with them:

$$\frac{\text{(VP) Fiscal Buyer}}{\text{(MGR) User Buyer}} = \frac{\text{(ATL) Fiscal Buyer}}{\text{(BTL) User Buyer}} \qquad \blacktriangleleft \cdots\cdots\cdots \textit{The Line}$$

BTL Value	ATL Value
Easy to Use	Advances a Corporate Initiative
Has the Right Features	Saves Time
Great Support	Lower Risk
Is Within the Budget	Has a Good ROI
Integrates with What I am Working With	Gives Us a Competitive Advantage
Makes Me Look Good	Adds Value to Our Company Brand

THE OUTCOME

The tools and tactics in this book will have you calling higher, getting quicker responses, negotiating with more confidence, and speaking the right language.

▶ You will prepare better.

▶ You will listen more.

▶ You will guide, not tell.

▶ You will ask, not instruct.

▶ You will lead, not follow.

▶ Your sale cycle time will decrease.

▶ Your average sales price will increase.

▶ You will win more deals.

Calling high is not the trick. Anyone can do that. *The trick is when you're there, what do you say?* How do you keep the executive's attention? And how do you coordinate that conversation with the pitch you're delivering below the line?

Welcome to *Selling Above and Below the Line*.

Acknowledgments

Where do you start when you want to thank those who have supported you as you worked on your book? Usually, authors list all the people who have contributed to its content, its ideas, and its context. In my case, those are a whole lot of people in the business world.

Then there are family and friends who have been supportive, and there are many. They add up with lot. When you are holed up for hours writing something like this, it's amazing how it disrupts other people's schedules.

So thanks to all, family and friends . . . you've been great.

Also, a personal thanks to the sales folks at Tableau. What a great culture. To the Infusionsoft team, it's been a super time.

To the folks at AMACOM: You really came through on this one. Thank you, Bob, Ellen, Michael, and the crew. Debbie: Every author should have a copyeditor as gifted and with a sense of humor as yours.

Hey Google, you definitely know the difference between I get it and "I get it!"

And it seems appropriate to acknowledge you, the reader, for a change. It's hard to break old habits. Reading this book and putting it into action is going to take courage and character. You have taken the first step by reading this book, and usually first steps are the hardest.

Create a support team. Have your manager coach you. Have another rep work with you. Heck, show your prospects what you are doing and ask for their help. Treat the advice in this book as though you are learning

French in an immersion program. Change will not happen unless you give it your all and don't look back. Cortez had it right.

Getting good at selling to both the BTL user and the ATL executive is a journey. You will learn and make mistakes along the way. Enjoy the trip. Ask for help. It's worth it.

CHAPTER *1*

You Are Selling More Than Just Features and Benefits

Carlos was confident. He had been in this position before, and he was on a roll. He stood at 142 percent of his quota YTD, and if he closed this deal, it would make his year, with three months to go.

"Do you think we have covered everything?" his manager, Jeanne, asked. "This looks good, but are you sure about tomorrow's meeting with the COO and CEO? This seems quite technical to me."

"It's good, Jeanne. They're both very technical people. The manager who they are relying on told me what to say. We've only got thirty minutes to explain to them why we are the best solution. I've cut out all the fluff and will present just the essentials on who we are, why we are uniquely qualified, and when this solution can be fully implemented."

"Okay, I'm trusting you. What role do you want me to play?"

"Just answer any questions they have. Let's work together on closing this deal tomorrow. I don't think they are going to ask for more than 15 percent off, and we're okay with that, right?"

"That's more than we like to give, you know that. Let's just see how this plays out."

Carlos did not get the sale. He was overly technical and did not address what the C-levels wanted. Relying on his User Buyer's information and guidance, he focused on features and benefits, and that was just not good enough for the executive suite. They wanted to hear numbers; how much time this was going to save on their current initiatives, how much cost or risk was going to be reduced. Right level, wrong language. Brought a knife to a gunfight.

Stories like this play out over and over again.

THE NEUROSCIENCE OF SELLING: IT'S ALL ABOUT US

The thoughts are familiar. You've played them over and over in your head countless times.

"If I can just get them to see our value proposition."

"If the prospect could just see it how we see it, they would make a decision for us in a heartbeat."

"We are the perfect fit for what they are looking for. What do we have to do to make them see that?"

It just feels good talking about us. It really does. For most people, our own thoughts and experiences are some of our favorite things to think and talk about. Research at Rutgers University shows that people spend 60 percent of their conversations talking about themselves—and that number rises to 80 percent when we're using social media platforms such as Twitter or Facebook.

Why do people, especially salespeople, spend the majority of their time talking about themselves and their solutions? Because it feels good. Research at Harvard University has shown an increase in neural activity in areas of the brain associated with motivation and reward when people are talking about themselves. It's the same area that lights up when we get gratification from happy experiences, good food, and sex.

In a sales situation, talking about yourself and your point of view—your features and benefits—is enjoyable. Those good vibrations make salespeople go on and on about themselves and their product's features and benefits, regardless of the complementary—and essential, it turns out—need to talk about the customer's problems and the resolution to those problems.

The bottom line is that talking about us—our products and the benefits they confer—is intrinsically rewarding. The research also showed it was rewarding even if no one was actively listening! Even posting information about ourselves on our social media outlets makes us happy.

In fact, many salespeople have had great success pitching features and benefits. And especially since they have enjoyed doing it, they have convinced themselves that it's the right thing to do.

However, the savvier among them know they leave something on the table. Why? Because features-and-benefits salespeople are rarely invited to the final meeting, the one where the User Buyer makes the final pitch to the executive team on the sales process, the preferred vendor, and the proposed final price, while the salesperson waits by the phone or out in the lobby.

Hey, even a blind squirrel finds a nut once in awhile.

THE DECEPTIVE LURE OF FEATURES AND BENEFITS

When sales teams fall prey to the fallacy that they can win sales with a focus on features and benefits, who is to blame?

▶ Marketing, since they jam product features and benefits down the sales organization's throats?

▶ Sales management, since they stress product knowledge, deal management, and key competitive land mines in presentations and demonstrations?

▶ Customers, since they drive the feature/benefit discussion with a decision criteria sheet?

▶ Salespeople, since they are have fine-tuned their feature/benefits presentation and receive glowing reviews from the User Buyers and bosses they present to?

It's a mix of all of the above.

Rather than lay blame for this shortsightedness on individuals or particular parts of the organization, let's instead consider the way things have always gotten done, and why. And why it's time for a change.

To get started, let's look at two sales scenarios and how they were addressed by two salespeople with very differing approaches:

Jill needed a new accountant for her business. She got some good recommendations and narrowed the candidates down to two, Larry and Diane. She made a visit to Larry's office to help her determine if he and his firm would be a good fit.

Jill walked into Larry's office. It was richly designed, with beautiful wood furniture and degrees on the wall. Larry started in.

"We've been in business for over thirty-three years. My father, John, started the business and we have a stellar reputation. We have been in the same location and have had many of our clients since day one. As a matter of fact, Bill Murphy is coming over this afternoon, and his company was one of our first.

"Jill, we aren't like a lot of firms who nickel-and-dime their clients. We treat our clients like family. You have an audit, we're right in there with you. We also keep you up on the latest tax and audit laws on a monthly basis. We know what our clients need, and we proactively are there for them."

Jill had an appointment with Diane later that afternoon. She had the same type of office with similar degrees on the wall.

"Thanks, Jill, for coming down. Before I get into who we are and what we do, could you please tell me what you are looking for in an accountant, and what would be two or three characteristics of the firm that would be important? Let's start with what happened that's causing you to look at changing what you have currently."

An hour later, Jill had defined what she was looking for. She did not hear a lot from Diane about her firm, but Diane really had it down about what Jill was looking for, and Jill felt she had been heard.

Frank was frantic. The expiration of his current lease had snuck up on him, and he needed to see if he could do better. The location was ideal, but the 25 percent rent increase the landlord, Jack, was asking for was hard to swallow. Frank met with Jack to see what could be done.

"Frank, my costs have skyrocketed," Jack said. "I've had to add a new maintenance guy, make a major investment in the phone and communication system, and I'm looking at having to resurface the parking lot. You'll really enjoy the new parking lot. The current one is such an eyesore. I can't wait, and I'm sure you and your car will appreciate it!

"I know 25 percent seems steep, but I've held these costs down for you the past couple of years, and now I'm paying for it. So I'm sorry, but I'm just trying to keep up with the times."

Frank then had a meeting with a building owner three blocks away. It was not a perfect location, but one that could work.

"Frank," said Phil, the building's owner, "moving locations is always an ordeal. 'How will my customers find me? How easy is it to switch the mail, phone, and Internet connections? How long do I have to be down? How much is it really going to cost me?' These and probably a bunch more questions are probably running through your mind. So let's discuss first things first. Why are you considering changing locations?"

What is the common thread between these two stories? In both, the first sellers talked about themselves—who they were and why what they offered would make a difference to the buyer. They both had a lot to say and wanted to make sure they were heard.

The second seller in each story just asked questions and listened to the buyer, prompting them to discuss what was motivating them to change, and what they were looking for from the change.

You probably picked up on this immediately. And, of course, if it's so obvious to you, it has to be obvious to the sellers—and buyers—as well. So why do so many people sell like the first examples and not the second ones?

I say there's something obviously missing with the features-and-benefits approach. What is it?

The majority of salespeople, regardless of what they sell, just have to deliver that features-and-benefits pitch. It happens on sales calls time and time again. But it turns out that what companies think their value proposition is to their customers may not be what the market thinks it is.

Product Knowledge Is Easy—and Insufficient

Let's get to the key variable. Why do most salespeople rely so heavily on their knowledge of their product's features and benefits? Is it possible that it's simply because it's just so easy and feels good? Let's tell everyone who we are and why we are so great (here's where you pump out your chest) and will conquer the world.

Marketing Value? Not Enough

Companies and salespeople believe in the marketing value of their organizations—who they are and what they stand for. It influences who they hire, their stock price, their competitive marketing decisions, and their product direction. So of course, companies believe that if prospects can get on board with their marketing value—why they are worth the price they are charging relative to competitive solutions—then the world is sane again.

This works . . . to a point.

Fiscal ROI Value? Something's Still Missing

The other side of this sale is the "business case," the return on investment (ROI), if you will. Regardless of features and benefits, any change, any decision, any purchase must make fiscal sense.

Returning to Jill's and Frank's stories, in each of them, the second seller was on the right path in asking questions to try to understand the business value the buyer was looking for. So let's assume that in both stories, those sellers got a lot of information from the buyer about what they were looking for, and why they wanted to change accounting firms, in the one case, and physical locations, in the other.

Great. Then what? After twenty minutes of questioning, does the seller then go into a features-and-benefits pitch on what they offer? Or is now the time to go into the fiscal justification for the prices that they will be charging? Neither; there has to be something more. Something's still missing as we try to get at the essence of selling beyond just features and benefits.

BUYERS BUY OUTCOMES

When you look at things from the customer's point of view, you will see two outcomes.

Outcomes are the WIIFM (what's in it for me) part of the sale. Customers usually hope for two outcomes for each sale:

Outcome #1: Whatever we buy will be better than what we have. It will be faster, lighter, quicker, brighter, superior, easier to use; it will also do more and be longer lasting. And I will be in charge of having to make this work. Call this outcome the "BTL (Below the Line) Outcome." Why "below the line"? Because it is meant to satisfy the people in the middle and lower end of the corporate hierarchy.

Outcome #2: What we buy will make us money, save us time, or lower our risk. It will assist in our need to change. It will move one of our top priorities forward this quarter by at least 20 percent. We call this outcome the "ATL (Above the Line) Outcome." Why "above the line"? Because this outcome must meet the need of the C-suite, at the top of the corporate hierarchy.

Here's the hitch. Both outcomes are of importance. However, salespeople generally spend more than 80 percent of their time selling only to Outcome #1 (all about what the seller can do for the User Buyer). When they finally try to address Outcome #2 (all about the customer and their initiatives), it's usually too late in the sale. So the whole sale rests on Outcome #1, or really, only one value proposition. That's an unnecessarily anemic basis for influencing a decision.

"It's not my job to tell them what to do with what we are selling them."

"Hey, they are the ones who gave us the decision criteria . . . what they are looking for. We can't tell them legally how much we are going to save them."

"My job is to explain the features and the benefits of what we sell, right?"

Why do salespeople only go after the BTL value proposition? It's what salespeople have been taught to say, taught to present, and taught to demonstrate and quote. It's also what prospects demand when they want to do a trial, have a specific request, or just come to the website and do some initial investigation. Well, if that's what they are curious about and want to spend money on, far be it from the salesperson to buck that trend.

So a sales approach can be all about BTL Outcome #1, which is not that bad. It does result in the articulation of a unique value proposition.

But you are leaving about 50 percent of the prospect's value proposition off the table, sometimes even more. That's a lot of value.

Why are you doing this? It's because you have had some success in sales without having to address ATL Outcome #2. Marketing hasn't told you about Outcome #2. Your sales manager has not insisted on getting two outcomes or value propositions identified in the sales process. Heck, everyone is talking about Outcome #1 anyway, so what's the big deal?

Well, let's look at what is really driving your actions—or should be driving them.

Here is a typical Customer Buying Process, which I define as unfolding in six stages (see Figure 1–1).

Stage 0: The need to change is identified. The customer identifies a need to change a process, a methodology, a current way of doing things at the C-level. Something is broken, or is going to break, and management needs to change the way they are doing things currently. This decision to change is very much driven by Outcome #2. At this point, Outcome #1 is really just along for the ride. The User Buyers would love to get their hands on something new and different. They hear rumors of something new, so they go to websites, kick tires, get free trials, and request demos so they can be prepared if their input is requested. There is, however, no energy to change the current business proposition.

Stage 1: The needed change is defined and refined. Once management (the ATL stakeholder in Outcome #2) has decided to change a process, a piece of equipment, or a way they are currently doing things, they turn the definition of the specific requirements over to the people who will be responsible for using the new equipment or method (Outcome #1). They will be the ones to decide if it can work. Management just makes sure they stay within a reasonable timeframe and budget.

Stage 2: The seller's product is evaluated. It's all features and benefits (Outcome #1) as the seller presents the product for an initial evaluation.

Stage 3: The product is demoed and validated. As the selling process moves through validating and demonstrating the product in greater

Figure 1–1 Customer Buying Process

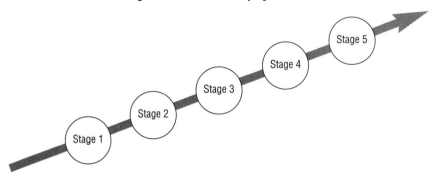

detail, features and benefits again take center stage. Management only needs to validate the premise, while the users need to validate that whatever they are evaluating will work, since they will be the ones whose jobs will be on the line.

Stage 4: Product costs are justified and the proposal is fine-tuned. During the period of justifying the expense and working out the fine points of the proposal, the appropriate focus is on Outcome #1, but management, most interested now in Outcome #2, will get involved to ensure the buyer gets the "best deal, and does not go over budget." (Note that Outcome #1 is under a budget limitation.)

Stage 5: A decision is made. When it's time for the final decision, lower-level management should be confident that agreement to the sale will result in Outcome #1. But now the executive suite gets involved to hammer out the best deal and to make sure that what has caused them to seek change in Stage 0 is actually being addressed by what they are getting in Stage 5.

What's the missing key ingredient? Simple. ATL Outcome #2. Where did it go? Why didn't sales engage with executive management as early as possible to find out why they have targeted this requirement as a top priority and put it into their budget? That conversation—about the buyer, not about the seller's feature/benefits—rarely happens.

Outcome #2 reflects a different value proposition, a different outcome from the one that focuses on the Outcome #1 buyer.

The typical sale plays out. Enter the hungry salesperson responding to an Outcome #1 inquiry, and it's off to the races. She doesn't even think about Outcome #2 until Stage 3 or 4. Well, that's leaving a lot of the customer value proposition out of the discussion. Why would you want to do that?

Great salespeople make sure they understand both of their buyers' value propositions, both of their desired outcomes as early as they can in the sales process. By addressing both outcomes early in the process, salespeople can realize:

▶ An increased selling price. The more value the prospect sees in the proposition, potentially the more money they will spend or the less they will concern themselves with a fixed budget.

▶ Since Outcome #2 is addressed early, the speed of the deal increases, and it is finalized more quickly.

▶ With a two-part value proposition, price negotiations at the end of the process are minimized.

▶ Since you have uncovered Outcome #2 in C-level language, you are now an asset to Outcome #1. You can help get them what they want.

▶ Addressing both outcomes gives you an obvious competitive advantage.

This two-part value proposition exists. You probably have made a sale involving both parts. The point is to be purposeful in addressing both outcomes, both value propositions, in sync with the *customer's buying cycle*, not your preconceived sales cycle.

You need to think like a customer and understand their process, not just how they will like what you're selling.

It's not all about you . . . yet.

CHAPTER *2*

The Line That Splits the Two Parts of a Sale

Companies need to grow profitably in order to survive. Stagnation or decline is never good for business. As they grow, adapt, take the lead, firm up, protect, and strive, companies are always moving. If a company isn't moving, like a shark it will surely die.

Companies also need to buy and sell, and when one company is buying, one is selling.

However, selling to a company is not always simple. As we saw in Chapter 1, smart salespeople sell two different value propositions, or outcomes. And they treat them as distinct outcomes, since that is how the customer sees them.

In a graphic illustration of these two value propositions, I insert a line between them. The BTL Outcome—Outcome #1—is below the line and geared to the User Buyer; it's the one salespeople seem to gravitate to. To sell to this outcome, salespeople focus on features and benefits; they trot out their detailed product knowledge and all the reasons they should be the selected vendor. And sometimes they win.

Satisfying the ATL Outcome—Outcome #2—requires selling above the line and is geared to upper management, and this typically escapes the sales team. ATL selling is about the return on the investment the company will make as they change what they are currently doing. Most salespeople believe this is an internal customer function, so they don't try to get invited to this party, and probably wouldn't know how to sell there if they did.

ATL Outcome

BTL Outcome

There is a line between the two outcomes as shown above, since they are so different. These two outcomes are rarely addressed in one presentation, and for a good reason: The two outcomes are desired by two very different audiences within the company—the User Buyer is working toward the BTL Outcome, and the Fiscal Buyer wants the ATL Outcome.

BUSINESS ACUMEN: KNOWING WHAT MAKES A COMPANY TICK

What is business acumen? Why is it so important to have it when you are selling? Easy questions, long answers.

When an individual within a business is either buying something or selling something, she's not doing it in a vacuum. Multiple people are involved, and usually multiple departments.

Let's look at ABC Watch Company, which wants to purchase a new truck for deliveries; Figure 2–1 shows us everyone who has to get involved with that one decision.

ABC Watch Company, in response to its Sales VP's forecast, believes it will exceed its sales targets by 20 percent this year. This makes the VP of Sales very happy. However, the VP of Engineering did not expect this extra work, especially with the sales team selling so many custom watches. The VP of Manufacturing also may have to add resources—another shift of workers.

The VP of Marketing is also involved now since the sales team needs more collateral and marketing materials. Let's not forget the VP of Finance, who has to set the new goals for revenue and management bonuses. Of course the VP of IT has to update the order entry system, and the VP of Purchasing has to buy all the additional equipment and services. And let's not forget the Manager of Delivery, who says that with-

Figure 2–1 ABC Watch Company

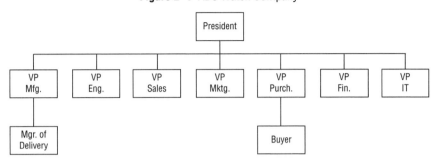

out a new truck, the inventory will be stuck on a dock and no one will make their management bonus; the Manager of Delivery told the Buyer to go get one, but learned there was no budget for that purchase. Yep, this is how a business works.

Of course, the President has to make sure all these changes align with the corporate goals everyone—management, investors, and employees—signed on for at the beginning of the year, and she must find the funding, based on the new sales numbers, to pay for the new truck.

Each of these employees of ABC Watch Company has a say in buying or leasing the truck to a certain extent. Obviously, the Manager of Delivery has a huge say. He has to make sure the truck:

▶ Fits in with the current fleet for maintenance proficiencies.

▶ Is easy to use and can be driven by current drivers.

▶ Comes with a GPS system that is compatible with the current IT system.

▶ Has the size needed to ship as many watches as possible yet can fit through the tight delivery dock alleyway.

▶ Comes with the extra-high storage capacity module to accommodate high-volume shipping times like Father's Day and Christmas.

Oh, and it has to come in under the $25,000 budget. These are all BTL value proposition features and benefits; if they are a good fit, the outcome sought by the BTL buyer (Outcome #1) is satisfied.

Then there's the management of the company. They have a different outcome requirement. Their expectation is that the cost of the truck should be less than the profits that will be yielded from the sale of the additional watches. The truck also needs to be very reliable, since the company runs without backup trucks and the consequences of a breakdown are huge. It needs to last at least five years and be large enough to handle growth that will take place during that time. Additionally, they cannot afford to wait the usual six weeks for delivery, since that would eat up at least 20 percent of the expected additional revenue (20 percent of $600,000 would be $120,000 at risk). This is management's desired outcome (Outcome #2): As long as the truck comes in between $25,000 and $30,000, and this cost can be amortized over five years, all is good, based on current profit ratios. Heck, with these additional revenue and profit numbers, they can even spend more if they need to.

UNDERSTAND A COMPANY'S NETWORK OF CONCERNS

What caused the company to decide it would have a 20 percent increase in revenue? Was it the Manager of Delivery saying they needed a new truck? Not hardly. ATL execs saw an opportunity to reforecast the sales and revenue for the company over and above the current forecast. Whatever the reason—a competitor's failure, market growth, increased demand, or their entry into new markets—their initial forecasts were too low; another possibility is that they were prepared to spend more money on marketing to get more revenue. If they forecast a 20 percent increase in revenue, they get more profits, which they can spend to invest in new growth.

Restated current year numbers that would give them additional capital budget to fuel growth will tend to yield additional assets for all departments, but we're just looking at delivery and its new truck.

Believe it or not, a new truck impacts the entire company. It affects marketing because they now have fewer limitations on where they can ship. It affects IT because if the new truck has a different GPS system, the current IT GPS routing system will have to be modified. Finance will have to get involved to get a new lease, and so on. This network of concerns exists in all companies, and a successful sale will address all or most of them.

TARGET TWO OUTCOMES FOR A SALES PROCESS THAT WORKS

In response to a 20 percent increase in sales, the company wants to grow an additional 20 percent. As one consequence, the BTL outcome has come into play and is going to make some truck salesperson very happy.

But an ATL outcome—investing so they can meet their 20 percent growth target—has come into play as well. ATL execs will consider a long list of investments and expenditures it will take to get to the 20 percent growth figure. Not all will be approved. Not all departments will get what they want. The ATL execs will look at the ones that help the company get to its 20 percent growth figure and will determine which ones have the best ROI.

The last thing the ATL execs want is a truck presentation. However, that's what the Delivery Manager has just scheduled and asked the ATL exec if he wants to attend. "Hmmm, how can I get out of that one?" he is asking himself.

How can we avoid this scenario? By examining the traditional sales process (see Figure 2–2) and transforming it into a sales process that works.

Figure 2–2 The Traditional Sales Process

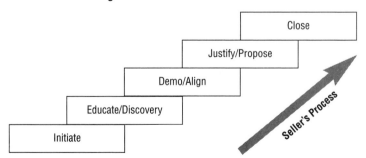

The Traditional Sales Process

To start at the beginning, let's say a lead comes to the sales department from a website hit or a cold call. You are in Stage 1. The salesperson or pre-salesperson has the initial conversation with the prospect and they are initially qualified with BANT (Budget, Authority, Need, Timeframe), MMM (Money, Method, Motivation), ANUM (Authority, Need, Urgency, Money), or some other initial sales qualification method. The salesperson determines that there is some initial interest and that the prospect is worth some more time, so the process moves to Stage 2, Education/Discovery.

At Stage 2, the salesperson does his best to determine if:

▶ The prospect has a need.

▶ The selling company can meet that need in a competitive fashion.

▶ The prospect has a budget.

That's about it. The goal at Stage 2 is to really find out what the prospect wants, determine whether the sales team can sell it to them, and figure out if they can sell it to them at roughly the amount the prospect has budgeted. If most of these criteria are met, the sales team moves the deal into Stage 3, the Demonstration.

This is when the prospect gets to see what they are buying in operation, be it a test drive in a car, swinging the new golf clubs, a software trial, or the results of an initial services engagement. The goal is to have the prospect see what they are going to buy *in operation* so they can "take ownership" of it. This an important step, since the sales team believes that if the demonstration goes well, they are in the home stretch.

If the demonstration goes well, it's on to Stage 4, the Proposal. This is the touchy part of the sale. If the price is too high, you may lose the sale. If it's too low, you may not give the prospect entirely what they want and you'll be seen as second rate. Negotiations could even spread to the purchasing department, which seems to only be in existence to beat salespeople up over price, regardless of quality and fit.

If this goes well, the deal enters Stage 5, Close, and the deal is finalized, with or without some loose ends that need to be cleared up, such as a credit check, final legal terms and conditions, etc.

There you have it, a traditional sales process. Ta-da!

What Happens in a Traditional Sales Process

In the conventional view, a sales process usually:

- ▶ Focuses on what the selling team has to do in some particular order.

- ▶ Includes sales activities, but rarely buyer activities. It's almost as though the buyer is just watching or is along for the ride as the selling organization goes through its paces.

- ▶ Is built so the selling team can conduct the process as quickly as possible.

- ▶ Usually stalls or goes dark near the end.

With a nod to Dan D., here is a good tongue-in-cheek version of a typical sales process (see Figure 2–3).

Figure 2–3 Dan D.'s Selling Process by Stage

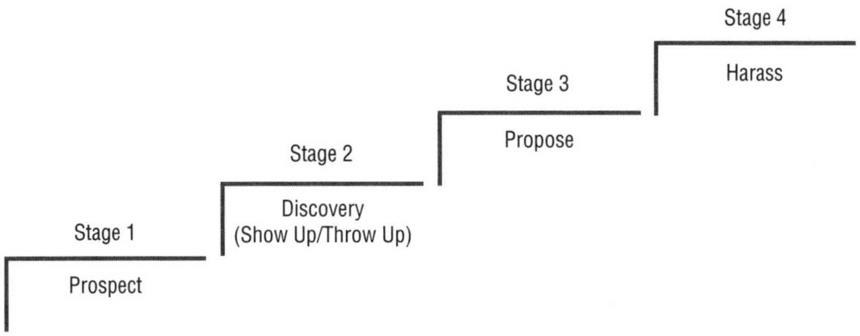

It starts off with Prospecting, then quickly gets to Discovery, which is where we force prospects to sit through slide after slide, white paper after white paper, and a discussion of feature after feature after feature.

Then it's on to the Proposal. Once that is delivered, the buyer has full control, so to get them to call us back, we have to graduate to the final step, Harass.

What's funny about this is it's closer to the truth than anyone cares to admit.

A Fresh Look at the Sales Process

Let's move on to consider a sales process that has five stages, but with some significant differences that make it more successful.

Stage 1, Initiation, is prospecting and some qualifying, either by marketing-generated leads or by warm or cold calling by the sales team.

In Stage 2, Education, the salesperson tells the prospect what the company does and why its product or service is uniquely qualified to satisfy the customer's need. At this stage, salespeople become educated about what the prospect is looking for (the *decision criteria*).

In Stage 3, Demonstration/Validation, the selling team attempts to prove they can do what they say they can do and to show how that aligns with the customer's needs. The team demonstrates the product or service and offers testimonials, or proofs of concept.

Stage 4, Proposal, is the first round of negotiations. The selling team lists one or more options that will satisfy the prospect's criteria.

Stage 5, Decision, is the final negotiation, which hopefully ends in a closed sale.

THE SPLIT: SELLING ABOVE AND BELOW THE LINE

An even better sales process works in a similar way, but the salesperson looks more deeply into the needs of the buyer and adds a special twist.

Stage 1 involves the necessary prequalification to determine need and fit. At Stage 2, salespeople are looking to educate the buyer on the features and benefits of what they offer. They also are doing the critical work of digging into the needs of the buyer.

However, the prospect does something at this stage—something selling teams often don't know about. At the buying organization, consideration of the sale splits at Stage 2. Depending on their role, people on the buyer's end start thinking about two separate outcomes: those that will happen above the line and those that will occur below the line. Whether the salesperson knows it or not, after the initial expression of interest, decision makers on the buyer's end now split into individuals or groups with two sets of concerns—the BTL Outcome and the ATL Outcome.

The Below the Line (BTL) buyer is the User Buyer, who appears to be driving this decision and is the person with the list of needs and the decision criteria. Since BTL buyers are the most affected by the day-to-day use of whatever is being sold, salespeople have a tendency to drop below the line as soon as they reach Stage 2. Why? Because all the BTL buyer wants to talk about is what salespeople are selling, which is what salespeople love and have been trained to talk about.

Above the Line (ATL) buyers look at a sale differently than BTL buyers, since they have different needs. Figure 2–4 illustrates the sales process for both the BTL buyer and the ATL buyer.

The ATL buyer has stated the need for a change that involves buying something, and this purchase is going to effect a value proposition in the

Figure 2–4 The ATL–BTL Split

The Cause/Effect Split

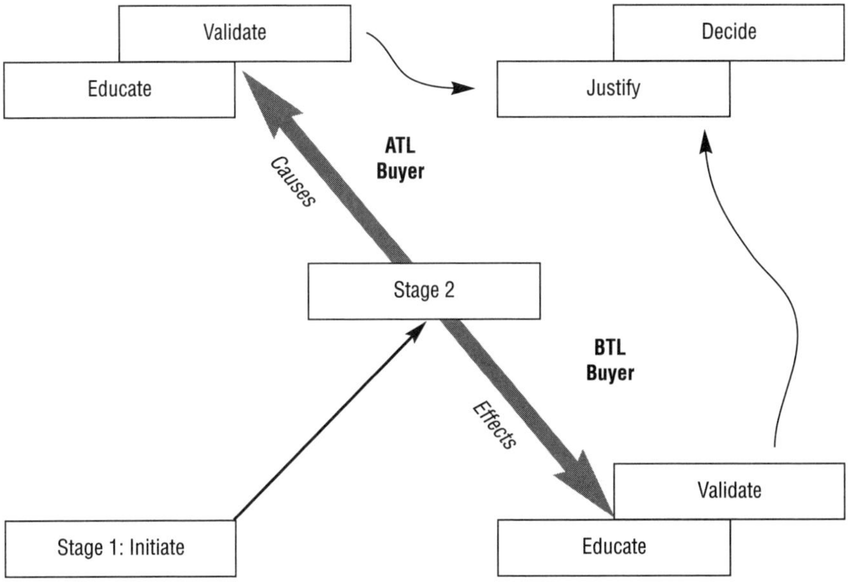

mind of the ATL buyer, so he gives the BTL buyer a budget and authority to proceed. However, the initial motivation for this sale lies with the ATL exec, who is the one who has to do or change something (for example, respond to a projected 20 percent increase in revenues).

Meanwhile, by Stage 2 the sales team has dropped below the line for the features-and-benefits show—and, boy, are they in their element; everything but balloons and clowns. It is what they have been trained for and have practiced over and over. However, when they do this, they make a decision to chase the BTL value proposition and ignore the ATL value proposition. They are going with what is familiar and less risky, since they know the features and benefits very well.

This big mistake will come back and bite them at Stage 4.

UNCOVER THE BUYER'S MULTIPLE PERSONALITIES

What most salespeople don't know is that by Stage 2, the buyer splits into multiple personalities. That's because different parts of the organization want to know two different things.

1. *Does your product/service fit our needs?* Is it what we are looking for? Can the truck fit into the alleyway? (BTL case)

2. *Does it contribute to making money, saving time, and/or lowering risk?* Can it contribute to the change we are implementing? Will one truck be enough to ship all we must manufacture to make the new revenue goal? (ATL case)

We call this split the Cause and Effect Split. What do I mean by this? *Effects* are a list of needs. They are very important to the BTL User Buyer, since it's these features and benefits that will determine which product or service he recommends. *Cause* provides motivation, the energy for the sale. It's what's causing the ATL to allocate resources and funds for this purchase.

Both parts of the split are important, and without addressing both of these points before you leave Stage 2 you are basically going forward with only one area of value instead of two, and why would you do that?

Let's look at how this happens

In a typical sale, the selling team gets to Stage 2, goes below the line, and dives into the practical needs. They match the User Buyer's stated needs with the features of the product or service. They showcase the benefits.

Then they head right for Stage 3, the demo, since this is where most salespeople believe they shine. You have a great demo, you validate that you can actually do what you said you can do, and the sale is as good as done.

You move to Stage 4 and offer the prospect a really good proposal. Things are looking good, and you are even forecasting success with this sale to your boss. You have the right product, have met the BTL decision criteria, and have momentum. What could go wrong?

The problem is that while you and the BTL buyer are at Stage 4, the ATL buyer—his value proposition unaddressed and unmet—is still at Stage 2, probably busy with other things. The ATL buyer has no idea that what you are offering can help with her outcome.

For this deal to reach a conclusion, the ATL buyer has to get to the same Stage 4 as the BTL buyer. When you're at Stage 4, typically one of two things takes place:

1. Your BTL buyer, with very little ATL knowledge and selling skills, tries to get the ATL buyer to Stage 5 all alone, without you.

2. Your BTL buyer asks you to accompany her to a meeting with the ATL buyer. You take this opportunity to present an "executive overview" of what you and the BTL buyer have been working on, and hope for approval and movement by the ATL exec to Stage 5. (Color photos of the new truck and how it can clear the alleyway.) But this presentation means nothing to the ATL buyer, except to see how excited the BTL person is. The ATL value proposition has not been discussed, so this sale is going to stall.

This deal is officially out of your hands, and it's now time to negotiate like crazy on price, push as hard as you can—and hope you get lucky.

Is this really what you want to keep doing?

FOCUS ON TWO VALUE PROPOSITIONS

So why isn't the customer getting back to you when they said they would? But it's only been a few days, and you are sure they are really busy.

Hey, the least they could do is quickly respond to your phone call or email with a status update.

Finally, you face it: Your deal has officially gone dark . . . quiet . . . ghost . . . silent . . . south . . . off the radar. You're not going to make the sale.

Why? What happened?

In a nutshell, you are paying the price of ignoring the separation of the buyer's concerns into the ATL Outcome and the BTL Outcome. The buyer is now in control of this deal.

Back at Stage 2, you should have understood that the buyer had two separate concerns and that in order to take control of the sales opportunity, you needed to honor that split. You needed to uncover the value propositions for the ATL buyer and the BTL buyer before you left Stage 2.

What most salespeople don't know is that the ATL buyer will see them at Stage 2. They will be happy to be assured, early in the sales process, about the validity of their assumptions—that is, that the purchase will contribute to the change they have initiated.

In most cases, the BTL buyer will not act as a blocker or a gatekeeper when you call on the ATL exec this early—and you know you must, since you have already spoken ATL language to the BTL buyer, and he had no clue what you were talking about when you asked:

"What are the reasons for you to implement this change?"

"What has happened that caused you to look at this?"

"What would be the impact this year if you did nothing?"

These questions are outside the scope of the BTL buyer, so you are now free to call on the ATL buyer, and thereby control The Split.
OK, this is a lot of theory and a lot to absorb. Take a breath. Now it's time to dig in and see what is really going on both below the line and above the line.

CHAPTER *3*

Selling Below the Line

Jerry had the deal. He had it.

Mark, the Manager of Engineering Services at the List Manufacturing Company, had just finished watching the demonstration of the new software with Jerry, the salesperson, and was really pleased.

"This new software you have really lives up to its billing. The new search method, the new user interface, and how quickly it got back to me on that one data point I requested . . . Jerry, it seems like this is going to be a great product for us."

Jerry can still hear what Mark said, although that was six days ago. Since then, nothing—not a return phone call, no reply to his three emails. Mark did respond to a text, saying he was busy and would get back in touch, but his note sure was short and didn't give a lot of information about what was happening.

Jerry reviewed Mark's decision criteria:

1. A more robust search method

2. A strong user interface that feels more intuitive

3. Speedier calculations

4. Compatibility with the company's financial systems

5. Scalability

According to Jerry's calculations, his solution scored a perfect five out of five. That was even before price entered into the picture, and he knew that was not going to be an objection, since the prices that were being discussed were well within Mark's budgeted amount. So why has Mark gone dark?

If Jerry doesn't hear something soon, he'll have to go over Mark's head, and that usually doesn't go well. What other options are there?

What Jerry did was base his sale on the prospect's BTL value proposition, which is usually based on features, functionality, and benefits. This is the way sales organizations have been run for years, and it probably will never go out of style.

"My dad was a salesperson, and he tells me things don't change much. A sale, is a sale, is a sale..."

"I've been selling for years now. Oh, I've picked up a few tips and tricks, but selling is selling."

"Selling is a numbers game. Get out there, make some presentations, qualify, demo, negotiate hard, and get the order. The more doors you knock on, the better your chance of success."

Do these statements sound like something you've heard before? News flash: Sales may not have changed, but the way buyers buy certainly has.

So why don't sales teams change and adapt to the two value propositions? If features-and-benefits selling is so limiting, why do sales teams still do it?

THE RATIONALE FOR FEATURES AND BENEFITS

Salespeople concentrate on BTL buyers for numerous reasons, most of which are tied to their paradigms of how they can be successful—in other words, their success patterns.

It's Why You Joined and Work for the Company

If you are like most people, you like where you work. You like the people, probably like your boss, and love the product/service you are selling. You think it is pretty good . . . probably the best in the market. And people who buy from you are great, and people who don't buy from you are stupid, right?

Why couldn't these non-buyers see what you offered was so far and away better than what they settled for? You did your job; in fact, you did a great job moving the deal though the sales process. You gave a great presentation, the demo was awesome, and you gave your best shot at the pricing. You even gave more than that at the last minute to try to close the deal.

So why did the prospect buy from the competition? You may have missed something, but it must have been that:

▶ The VP had a preexisting relationship with the other firm.

▶ The RFP was heavily weighted away from your strongest features.

▶ The prospect minimized what your product does better than everyone else's. They said it wasn't that important to them. Really? It seems to be important to everyone else on the planet.

▶ They just didn't like you.

In other words, you have a supreme faith in your company and still work there because you believe in what you sell. You have the best features and service, good price points, and one of the best value propositions in the industry. If your prospects could just see what you see, they would never give the competition an appointment.

It's Competitive

Don't you just love winning? You were brought up in a competitive environment. Through sports, academics, siblings, and even being competitive with your parents, you were raised to compete.

It's that same drive that got you this sales job. You showed your boss, who hired you, that you have "the right stuff," that you rarely back down from a fight, and that you have what it takes to win. Well, if everyone is going to make this a competitive situation, then you need to identify the enemy, and that would be the competition.

Competitors lie, cheat, and shave the truth, and their solution is so far beneath yours that it should be easy for the buyer to notice the difference and select your offering.

The problem is, they don't buy from you all the time. As a matter of fact, when it gets really competitive, it comes down to price, and that's really not a great strategy, since the competition, what with their inferior, bargain-basement product, can go so much lower than you can.

However, when you beat them, it's so much fun. Your features and benefits, when you present them and the customer understands them, are a thing of beauty! You know your stuff cold, you know what the competition can't do, so you can position your solution in the best possible light (avoiding land mines) . . . and win. Man, you are at your best.

Boot Camp

So what did they teach you in your first few weeks of being employed with the company? Did they send you to a new-hire training class or a ramp class? Some actually call it sales boot camp.

This is where you get bombarded with all the things your company does:

▶ The company's history, products, and services

▶ The current executives

▶ The competitive benefits

▶ Your target markets

▶ A sales process that correctly positions the presentation and the demonstration

▶ Pricing and contract guidelines

▶ . . . all the BTL information you will ever need to win at the BTL level

Marketing Input

Marketing adds input to the BTL pile. Marketing collateral, marketing positioning information, analyst positioning information, market growth information—all are geared for you to sell to the BTL buyer. Everything you will need, from slides to customer referrals, data sheets, and instruction in how to conduct a successful demo, are handed out at the sales boot camp—and more. Marketing loves working for you, and they are helping . . . helping you have conversations regarding the BTL value proposition.

Boss's Pressure to Meet Goals

Let's not forget the sales manager and VP of Sales and their weekly and monthly strategy sessions. You better have a good handle on "the deal"— what you are selling, how you are going to sell it based on the value you are providing, how you position your solution against the competition— and of course, making sure it comes in by the end of the month or the quarter.

It's What They All Talk About

Walk the hallways of any sales organization. Are they talking ATL stuff? Of course not. What have you been trained on? How do you get promoted? Talking features and benefits gets you into the club. Which club? The club of "I know my products and features better than most other salespeople" club, as well as the "I have earned the respect of others" club, naturally. That club.

They Reward You When You Talk About the Company

Ask any salesperson about a deal. They can tell you what they sold, who they sold it to, how much they sold it for, which competitors they beat, and how they pitched their product/service in the best fashion possible.

But ask these same salespeople about their customers: annual revenues (actual and goal); margin goals; top initiatives and how your solution can help; future goals and how your partnership is going to make the adoption of a variety of initiatives easier. Hmmm. Most salespeople will be stumped.

You "Know the Business" if You Talk about Us and Not the Customer

The final reason that you are a benefits-and-features seller is that salespeople are rewarded, promoted, and seen as a valuable asset if they talk about the company and what it offers, rather than the customer. And this is what has to change!

TWO SALES PROCESSES, TWO RESULTS

Let's look at how two salespeople sold a new software system to the Jones Company.

Selling Below the Line: Looking at Half the Value

Tom, the sales manager, called in his best sales rep, Mark, to go over his forecast for the month. Tom was close to making the quarterly number, and needed the Jones deal to put him and the team over the top.

"Okay, Mark, tell me, what's the latest with the Jones deal?"

"Tom, I think we got this one. Should come in this week."

"Let's go over where we are with the account. I don't want to leave any stone unturned."

"Happy to. You know we started this about two months ago, when I called in to Jones and started a relationship with Paul Suggs, the senior manager of IT applications. Paul and I went through the list of what he was looking for. He really liked our user interface and our look-back feature, said it was going to really help him figure out his daily schedule, which it should. He also loved the fact that it can run in under an hour. Those are the two key things that I think hooked Paul for sure.

"Also, the demo we did for them went perfectly. Kate did a great job, and we are now looking at a deal of $120K, which is a bit over their budget, but Paul felt confident he could get the extra funds.

"The last time I talked to Paul, two days ago, he said he thinks we can get this signed off by this Friday. That's where we are right now."

"What about the competition? What are they doing with this account?"

"I know there is competition, and I know they are a bit cheaper than we are, but Paul has told me he likes us better, and he didn't seem too worried about them. I'm always thinking about the competition, but I think we're okay here."

"Do we need to call the VP of IT Services . . . what was his name . . . Lee Nagel, I think? We talked to him once a while ago. Wouldn't hurt to call."

"I think we're okay. Lee seemed a bit bored during the demo. I called him right after, and he said it looked good. He also said Paul was the guy who was going to use this, so I don't think he cares which system they buy, as long as Paul's happy. Also, I don't want Paul to think we are going over his head. Let's see how this plays out."

Selling ATL and BTL: Bringing the Full Value Picture into Focus

Meanwhile, at the competition, sales manager John called Gail into his office. The same Jones deal was also a key to making the quarter for both her and the team.

"So, Gail, what's happening with the Jones deal? Let's go through what we know and where we are."

"No problem, John. We started in Stage 1, when I called into Lee Nagel, the VP of IT Services. He told me there was a project going on that we might be a fit for, and sent me to Paul Suggs, his applications manager. Before I went to see Paul, Lee and I talked about:

▶ How he is losing 10 to 15 percent of his monthly productivity because of a lack of new systems.

▶ A new plant coming on line has taxed his resources. He had requested three new people, but the submitted budget doesn't seem to account for that. He thinks he'll get just one new person, and that's not enough.

▶ His current system is on its last legs, and the fact that we are willing to transfer all the old data to a new system at no additional charge is going to save him three weeks of time and not make a dent in the $15K budget he had allocated for the data transfer.

▶ He thinks he can get budget for one new person and $100K for a system like ours.

▶ He needs this up and running by the end of next month, which means he needs to make a decision this week, or next week at the latest.

"Lee and I came up with answers in three major areas: the productivity issue, the transfer of data issue, and the headcount problem."

"Great. How about Paul?"

"Paul had a list of seven key things he needed to see a system do. We can do six of the seven, and with our new release due out in the summer, we should be able to handle that last issue.

"At Stage 3, we made sure Paul saw how our product can handle what he needs to do, and had a thirty-minute phone discussion with Lee about how the product would directly benefit his initiatives, and to let him know that Paul was comfortable with our solution.

"We are now in Stage 4, and have gone over a few options with Lee and Paul. Paul wants the most expensive option, of course, but I think we are all going to settle on the $120K option that both Lee and Paul like, though obviously for different reasons.

"Lee seemed very relieved that Paul thought we could do the job. Lee just did not see the [competitor's] system having the same ROI for his issues as we do. Lee said Paul's final paperwork is due on his desk this Friday. That's where we are."

Do I Have to Tell You Who Will Make the Sale?

How many times have you been in the first situation, reviewing the deal with your boss and talking BTL stuff, and focusing on your features and benefits to the BTL user? Even if an ATL person comes into the discussion, as one person did for the demo, all that's really discussed are BTL features and benefits.

It's hard to really say who will get the sale, but it does look like Gail is addressing both value propositions, and not just the BTL user's needs. Can Mark make the sale? Sure he can, but Gail is in a much stronger place, and if you were to place a bet, the odds are definitely in Gail's favor.

In the vast majority of selling situations, you need to look at both ATL and BTL and get both value propositions. They are likely to be very different, but the two are equally important. You should never try to give a proposal to your prospect unless you have both of them nailed down.

BTL selling is important. It's very important for a deal to close. However, it should not be the only value proposition you chase. With that said, let's see what really is of importance to the BTL buyer.

WIIFM: THE FIVE Ps

"What's in it for me" is the rallying cry of the BTL buyer. It *is* really all about them, and that's as it should be. BTL buyers are the ones who are going to have to make what you are selling work. They will be held responsible for the results, good and bad.

And this purchase stands to make their life easier since it solves a problem, it will give them a good addition to their resume if they ever need to look for a job, and, what the heck, it's something new and different and will bring them quite a bit of attention in the company at large; when promotion time comes, it won't hurt to have been involved in this purchase.

Thus the BTL buyer is very WIIFM-focused on features and benefits. I like to classify what is important to them as the Five Ps, five key areas that the BTL User Buyer looks at when contemplating a purchase: Product Features, Perceived Quality of Fit, Professional Support/Ease of Use, Price to Value Ratio, and Personal Win.

Product Features

These are what the product or service does—what you are proud of, what you need more of to battle the competition. The BTL buyer is pushing hard for the latest and greatest. And why not—they don't want last year's model! They want to be on the cutting edge. When they make themselves indispensable to their boss and the company, their own value takes off.

Perceived Quality of Fit

This is the perceived quality of the product and service being offered. Judgment is in the eye of the beholder. So is quality. Quality can take so many different shapes and forms:

- Quality of fit
- Quality of service
- Quality of the vendor itself
- Quality of the sales approach
- Quality of expected value
- Quality of performance
- Quality of documentation
- Quality of integration
- Quality of the proposal

With so many variables, it's hard to know what the BTL buyer wants unless you ask. What they perceive as quality and you perceive as quality may be different, but in whatever form, quality is very important to the BTL buyer. They don't want to be associated with something that is not up to their standards and perceived needs, which is why their definition of quality is important to understand.

Professional Support/Ease of Use

Related key considerations are the perception of how easy the product is to learn and adapt to, and the amount and speed of the support the product requires. There is a learning curve for almost anything new—a new computer, a new car, even a new pair of shoes. To the BTL buyer, who is responsible for making this work, getting up to speed and knowing she can get help fast when she has a problem or question is important. She will judge support in many different ways, and will look at price vs. support levels when making a decision.

Price to Value Ratio

There needs to be a correlation between the value the prospect is getting and the budget the buyer has been allocated. The BTL buyer wants to get the most he possibly can for what he has to spend. The BTL buyer's ROI is based on features and benefits for their perceived value. Perceived value to the BTL buyer is based on what the new product or service can do for him, whether it be to eliminate a problem or make his job easier.

Personal Win

The final P is how this purchase will make the BTL buyer or the company look to his peers and superiors. Make no doubt about it—they want it to make them look good. BTL buyers, the ones who are going to use it, need to be really proud of what they have bought and are eager to show it off to all their coworkers. They win by getting the new toy. The company has invested in them, along with the product, and they love the attention and responsibility.

The product or service you are selling to the BTL buyer is going to help define them to their coworkers, their boss, and themselves. They need a win. You need to make sure you really understand this fifth P—the *personal win*—since it can be so important to the BTL buyer. It is how they are going to be identified, and to many, image is everything.

THE BTL BUYER'S MANTRA: I NEED IT AND I LIKE IT

The BTL buyer's attitude can be summed up in these words:

▶   I'm responsible for making whatever we buy work.

▶   I probably won't get a second chance at this.

▶   I'm the only one who really knows what we need.

▶   It has to do what I want it to do.

▶   I have to be able to use it, understand it, and be the expert at it.

▶   If I get in trouble, I better be able to get help.

▶   I want this to be important to the company, so I'm seen as a hero.

As a salesperson, you play into this. They are talking about your product and service, about you—your favorite topic. This is too good to be true. Salespeople feel good when they can talk about what they know and have the prospect agree and hang on their every word.

So let's go back. This "talk about us" mentality is also supported by the marketing, sales management, and executive management functions of Jerry's company. Remember Jerry, the salesperson at the beginning of this chapter, selling that new software? Jerry's company preaches to Jerry and their other salespeople that:

▶   We have the best products.

▶   We have great customers who like us.

▶   We have great customers who like using our stuff.

▶   Our testimonials say how much our customers like using our stuff.

▶   We have the best competitive product.

▶   We have the best service for our product.

▶   Our products have the best (BTL) value.

With all this BTL emphasis, how does Jerry or any salesperson learn that there is more to a sale than BTL value? Unfortunately, the answer is that they don't. They stay at the BTL level.

The BTL buyer is important, and by following the company line and doing what you have always done, you can often sell to the BTL what they really are looking for, but you are only getting at 50 percent of the potential value the prospect is attaching to this sale.

THE THREE LEVELS OF A PURCHASE

A final qualification for this approach into the ATL/BTL world of sales is in order. One size never fits all, so if you want to zoom in on what kind of sales this methodology can be useful for, read on. Let's assume there are three levels of purchasing in the sales world, and each has its own value proposition.

Level 1: Buying for Yourself

When you want to buy something for yourself, you are at the first level. You are usually the ATL and BTL buyer at the same time. You see something you think you want or need, tell yourself it's really what you want, validate, justify, and then make a decision. You may get some outside opinions, but the entire buy/sales process is yours. You bought the product or service to use; you justified it and made a decision. Examples would be when you buy a car, a new power tool, or a new printer.

Level 2: Purchase with Permission

The second level is when the person who is going to use something needs permission from someone or something, like a committee or stakeholder, in order to buy it. The person granting the permission really is not interested in the purchase, since it is reasonable and customary. Many schools and government agencies act in this way in their day-to-day purchases. Another good example is maintenance services. Level 2 purchases are things that show up year after year in annual budgets and rarely change.

Level 3: Selling Two Value Propositions

The third level is where both the ATL and the BTL buyer have a stake in the purchase. Each buyer has her own value proposition, and both can be used to justify the sales decision. Usually the salesperson gets one or the other, but both are available to the salesperson, and usually the two are quite different.

At this third level of buying, both value propositions are out there for the taking. The salesperson who can address both—satisfy the two value propositions—can justify the decision, beat the competition, and do it in less time and with less discounting.

Teaching you how to hone in on the ATL value proposition is just about the most important thing you will learn from this book.

COMPANY WIN AND PERSONAL WIN

Another way to look at this is as two perspectives: a company win perspective and a personal win perspective. A company win is usually an ROI, measured in dollars, time, risk, or perception. It really has nothing to do with what is being sold.

A personal win usually goes to the User Buyer, the BTL person, since they will be using what is being sold to their benefit. It will make their life easier and their job better; it will save them time or add value to their current job—and it will look good on their record.

Either way you look at it, the BTL buyer is usually heavily involved, but the BTL Outcome shouldn't be allowed to dominate the sale, however, since it's only half of the total value proposition.

ATL buyers also have a personal win in this game. It is more centered around how the product/service is helping them reach their objectives, minimize their problems, or get rid of the obstacles that are stopping them from hitting their objectives, rather than on just the product itself. ATL buyers have their own value proposition, and if you don't address it early, you will be left with half the value of the sale not being included in your value proposition. And then come the discounts and being treated like a commodity.

It's time to stop this and see what the ATL exec really wants.

CHAPTER *4*

Know Your ATL Buyer

The C-suite is where the energy is, where the money is, where the decision is. The problem is that most salespeople don't know what to do when they get there.

The Above the Line (ATL) buyer has a value proposition that most salespeople don't address. This chapter will help you understand what you are leaving on the table, and how you can address the ATL value proposition.

The ATL buyer is coming at the problem from a fiscal point of view, an investment point of view. Whatever they invest in must have an ROI. It must contribute to something that brings value to the company and their own initiatives.

Think about the department head the BTL works for. No doubt she has different goals and problems than the people she manages, right? If she has different goals and problems than the BTL buyer, then it stands to reason that she has a different value proposition, a different way of thinking about where she is going to spend her time and her money.

Your sale must bring some value to the ATL buyer. The BTL buyer is ready to start using what you are selling, but when you visit with ATL buyers, you need to focus on their:

▶ Initiatives ▶ Goals

▶ Fire drills ▶ Challenges

▶ Competitive threats   ▶ Management by objectives (MBOs)

▶ Experiments

ATL executives tend to have their goals and initiatives planned out and in process. Why would a C-level executive and/or a department head try to do something different than what he or she already has in process? Because their goals, initiatives, and MBO process are incomplete or involve more risk than they initially thought or will not bring home the expected results. Plans may need to be altered because of:

▶ Competition

▶ A change in the market

▶ Erroneous initial thoughts

▶ Loss of a team member

▶ New midterm goals

▶ Product problems

▶ Distribution problems

▶ Customer satisfaction problems

▶ IT infrastructure problems

▶ And an endless list of other potential variables . . .

Since executives are under enormous pressure to attain their goals and/or put out fires, they eliminate things that are blocking their success. The bottom line is that they *have* to change.

They have to change way they thought they were going to get it done, and they have to change the way they have always done it, perhaps in a way they never thought possible.

CHANGE: WE ALL FACE IT, AND WE ALL FEAR IT

People hate to change. Organizations hate to change. You hate to change. ATL people hate to change. Does "If it ain't broke, don't fix it" ring a bell? We'd *all* rather muddle along, doing what we've always done.

"We've Always Done It This Way"

An executive I know was a company turnaround expert. He would go into companies that were not performing well and try to turn them around to become profitable revenue growth companies. He told me that when he would go into a company that was not performing well, and he was expected to get it back into good health and back on track, he would always hear three comments from the current employees:

"We have always done it this way."

"We tried that a few years ago and it didn't work."

"You really don't understand our company and the industry. Once you do, you'll understand why we do the things we are doing."

He said once he showed the employees how resistant they were to change, and made them realize that there were no penalties to trying something new, they finally became open to change, since it sure beat what they were doing now.

"Excuse Me, You're in My Seat!"

We do two-day seminars all the time. To show the salespeople and sales managers they need to be open to change, we do two things.

On the first day, right after lunch, we ask a few of the attendees who come back early from lunch to change seats for the afternoon. In many cases they grumble, look confused, or try to figure out which would be the best seat to take. A few minutes later the rest of the attendees come back from lunch, and the people whose "old" seats are now occupied by someone else start complaining.

"Excuse me, you're in my seat!"

Instead of looking at this as a new opportunity to sit with some other people and gain different insights, they don't want to give up what is known and comfortable.

At the end of the first day, we ask the local attendees—usually the majority of the participants—to take a different route when traveling from home to the class the next day. We usually hold classes at the main office of the customer, so we are essentially asking the attendees to take a different way into work in the morning. We hear:

"Why? What's wrong with the way I've been going?"

"That's stupid. The way I come to work is the best way."

"I'll be late, and I'll mess up my whole day."

All we are asking them to do is take a different way into work, so they can see things differently. They may find something they never knew existed. They may find a oddball little shop or an exotic restaurant . . . the possibilities are endless.

Nah, they won't do it. Usually only one or two actually do it, and they usually get laughed at. Change is hard.

When Circumstances Force a Change

Nate had a great relationship at one of his client's headquarters with Daisy, Lynn, and Kelly and was really optimistic about next year's contract. He had had a meeting two days earlier where all three had said the contract should grow about 20 percent next year. This would put it over $1 million for the first time. With only thirty days to go before the end of the year, he should start off next year with a good head start.

As usual, he got into the office bright and early and started checking his emails. He opened one from Daisy only to find out that she and Lynn had been promoted and transferred to another division, effective immediately, and that Scott had been named new acting head of the department. Now this was a problem, since Scott had come from a competitor, and a few months ago was the lone voice to strongly speak out against the way Nate saw next year's contract shaping up. This could be—no, *will* be—a problem. Nate is going to have to change his selling approach and his ideas if he is to have any hope of expanding—maybe even retaining— the contract next year.

Sometimes, people who hate to change have something happen that forces them to change.

There are many reasons why people hate to change. There's that big one though, that gets people's attention right away—fear.

THE FEAR FACTOR

Change has a lot to do with fear. Fears are a major source of why people do not like to embrace change. We're fearful about what will result.

"Danger is real, fear is a choice."
—WILL SMITH

As part of his classic *Think and Grow Rich*, the great writer on success Napoleon Hill did an excellent study of what he called the fears of man. He classified and detailed the behaviors that result from each:

1. Fear of poverty
2. Fear of criticism
3. Fear of ill health
4. Fear of loss of love
5. Fear of old age
6. Fear of death

Perhaps the largest fear of all is a fear of poverty, exhibited in symptoms like letting others do the thinking, fault-finding, and procrastination. Fear of criticism can lead to indecisiveness and nervousness. Hill also talks about the fear of ill health, fear of loss of love, fear of illness, and fear of old age and death.

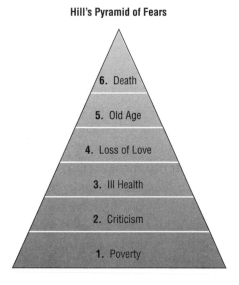

Hill's Pyramid of Fears

6. Death
5. Old Age
4. Loss of Love
3. Ill Health
2. Criticism
1. Poverty

In addition to the fears described by Napoleon Hill, I propose two fears that one sees in many salespeople and sales executives:

▶ Fear of the unknown   ▶ Fear of failure

Fear of the unknown leads to a lack of confidence, to an unwillingness to accept a challenge that involves risk. People who fear the unknown are afraid to try something that has never been done before—or that *they* have never done before; they think it will create more problems than the current situation. Fear of the unknown includes a fear of making the wrong decision and a fear of unknown outcomes.

Fear of failure may be the fear that encompasses all the fears discussed above. We fear becoming a big loser. No matter what choice we make, it will be the wrong one. We will be laughed at and be seen as someone who is never to be trusted again. We'll become a social pariah with no respect from friends and coworkers. The boss will never give us a second chance. Try as you might, you won't get the sale.

PROMOTE THE POSITIVE MOTIVATORS

Cause is a word that implies motion, that is, a change in place or position. It is a key word for a salesperson to ponder when calling on the ATL executive, since it implies an action is being taken. A definition of the word is a good place to start.

CAUSE, noun

1. something that produces an action or condition; motive, justification, or grounds for doing, thinking, or feeling something.

2. a principle, aim, or movement that a person believes in deeply and is prepared to defend or advocate.

What does the word *cause* make me think about as I ponder the problem of change?

▶ *Reason*—There is a purpose, an aim.

▶ *Motivation*—There is movement, action, or doing.

▶ *Drive*—There is a goal in mind.

Find What Will Cause Forward Motion

Change is based on a cause—a reason, a drive, and a motivation to do something different. And that begs the question, what would cause an ATL buyer to change what they are doing today? Most likely, it is their desire to get on the right track so they can accomplish their goals and objectives and those of their organization.

Cause creates an urgency and injects a timeframe into your circumstance. Without cause, you are living in a two-dimensional world, one defined by features and benefits—the world of the BTL buyer.

BTL buyers are in "fix it" mode. They have a problem, it needs fixing, and they will go all out to get the product/service to solve the problem—and all will be good.

It's like when something goes wrong at your house. A light bulb goes out; you need to fix the kitchen drawer; it's time to fertilize the lawn. The problem is immediate, and you need to go to the hardware store, buy the items you need to solve the problem, go home, and fix the thing that is wrong or broken. Do that, and all is good; you are acting in a two-dimensional buying world—buy it/fix it. There is a current need, the time is now. Fix the problem, and project accomplished.

ATL executives live in a different world, a three-dimensional world. Their world has a third dimension, which is time.

Time has three elements—past, present, and future—and only the first and the last have motion, or energy. This is where the ATL exec lives, in the past and in the future.

Comfort

Many ATL executives are comfortable with the way they are doing things; even if they know that what they are doing is not going to get them the results they desire. It's how they got to where they are at, and those success patterns are hard to give up.

The terms *conformation bias* and *belief perseverance* describe the situation in which people tend to hold on to their beliefs even when it appears that they should change. Everyone has tried to change someone's belief or opinion, and it's usually harder than most people think.

Over a third of corporate change initiatives fail, and more than half of employees feel bored in their jobs and believe their job advancement opportunities are limited. People are bored and don't want to do anything about it, and corporate change programs have limited success. Sound familiar?

So when ATL executives need to make a change, they are going up against a lot of fears, doubts, and uncertainties; they are attempting to change practices that feel familiar and that they are comfortable with. Yet the evidence in so many cases is overwhelming: What they are doing now is not working. They *must* change, yet they are fearful of the risks involved in change.

The number-one issue for managers we meet is the desire to make decisions more quickly, especially personnel decisions. More specifically, they wish they were willing to get rid of unproductive workers earlier. But they are afraid to bite that bullet because if they let that person go, it may take forever to replace him, and they may lose the headcount, so it's better to have someone who is performing at 70 percent than no one at all. Fears cause the manager to accept unacceptable behavior, to fail to change, and then to rationalize their decision.

A good salesperson must know how to help the ATL exec overcome this fear of change, this aversion to doing something different. This book will show you how.

What's in It for Me?

For the most part, in order to embrace change, ATL executives have to see an advantage for themselves and for the organization. In most cases, since it's their initiatives and goals that they control, there has to be something in it for them. What's in it for me (WIIFM) is a reason to change. When there is no WIIFM, the motivation to change becomes less and less, since it does not tie back into what's important to them.

If you can help them see their WIIFM (address their ATL Outcome), you will help motivate change.

On a BTL Call, Show Off the Latest/Greatest

It is the job of a BTL User Buyer to make sure the ATL exec is kept current when something new or different is being offered that can have an impact on the BTL's current job, tasks, or commitments or on how current processes are accomplished.

And sometimes a BTL User Buyer can become so passionate about the prospect of change that he can also get the ATL exec excited and able to see new possibilities. He shows the boss something critical to the BTL level that also indirectly impacts the ATL exec's realm. Sometimes the ATL exec will take action by way of the enthusiasm of the BTL User Buyer.

But such considerations—making ATL execs feel comfortable with change, appealing to their sense of WIIFM, and getting a boost from the BTL buyer—pale in comparison to the power of understanding the differences in the ways ATL and BTL buyers perceive time.

TIME ZONES: GREAT SALESPEOPLE ARE TIME-TRAVELERS

Of the three time zones—past, present, and future—only two have importance to the ATL exec. I've developed a tool to illustrate this concept (see Figure 4–1).

The first time zone is the past. ATL buyers will spend money, time, and resources on getting things back to where they were before all the changes and problems hit. They want to get rid of all their problems. They seek to be restorative.

No one—absolutely no one—wants to do worse in the present than in the past:

▶ You will spend $300 to get your computer running like it did before it started slowing down.

▶ Companies will spend huge sums to get a turnaround company back up to expectations.

▶ ATL executives will spend time and energy to get its sales force selling as they did before the recent slump.

The second important realm of time in the world of the ATL exec is the future: They are willing to invest in something now if it will pay big dividends down the line. ATL executives are always hanging out in the future.

You'll hear them say:

"We need to make this investment for next year's growth."

"There's no way we can make the second half of the year without this investment."

"There's big trouble coming next year. We need to invest now so we can ride out the storm."

Figure 4–1 Time Zones

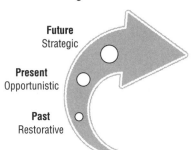

Future
Strategic

Present
Opportunistic

Past
Restorative

What happened to the present? Of course, it is still a time zone that ATL buyers are aware of, but it is of far less importance to them than it is to BTL buyers.

The present is where BTL buyers live. These buyers are tasked with making decisions on investments that will let the organization take advantage of a present opportunity.

You'll hear them say:

"There's a new tool out there right now that we can take advantage of."

"Our top competitor just went out of business."

"There's a three-day sale we should not pass up."

BTL buyers think more about the present, about today. They are given a task to do, and a short window of time to do it in; they need to fix things, so their focus is in the present. "I need to solve this problem my boss has given me, and I need to do it right now, since I really can't do my job without it."

QUESTIONS FOR A BTL OR ATL BUYER

"Ms. Wright, what is your most time-sensitive decision today?" (BTL)

"Ms. Brown, what decisions are you looking at over the next few months that are the most critical?" (ATL)

"Mr. Smith, what are some of the time-sensitive issues you had to face in the first part of the year that you really don't want to have to face again in the second half?" (ATL)

ATL executives hang out in the past and the future, so I like to think of talking with them as engaging in Time-Travel. They live where there is cause and where there is motion, where there is causal energy. Salespeople tend to be feature/benefit, two-dimensional, fix-it people. They like to fix things. When they help a customer fix a problem, they get rewarded with a sale. That's why they get along so well with the BTL buyer.

ATL execs try to avoid the mistakes of the last three to six months, or trying to make sure the next three to six months are smooth sailing. Salespeople, who come from the two-dimensional world of the BTL buyer, call on them and ask them a question that's based in the present:

"So, Mr. Smith, what's the biggest challenge you are facing right now?"

"So, Mr. Wright, what is keeping you awake at night?"

And the execs don't know. They are not thinking about today. Challenges and problems based in the past and extending into the future they get, but today? "Today" throws them for a loop.

The Right-Hand Rule

In engineering, there is something called the right-hand rule. It is a visual anchor for understanding vectors in three dimensions—X, Y, and Z. It's a helpful guide for engineers working in three-dimensional space, rather than a two-dimensional flat drawing.

Taking some liberty, we have modified this rule to illustrate the differences between two-dimensional and three-dimensional selling, that is, selling below and above the line (see Figure 4–2).

TWO-DIMENSIONAL QUESTIONS/COMMENTS

"Why are you looking at our product/service today?"

"What are the things you are looking for this solution to do?"

"Of the list of requirements you said you really need, which ones are the most important?"

"The demonstration today will focus on what you would use the system for right now."

Figure 4–2 Two-Dimensional vs. Three-Dimensional Selling

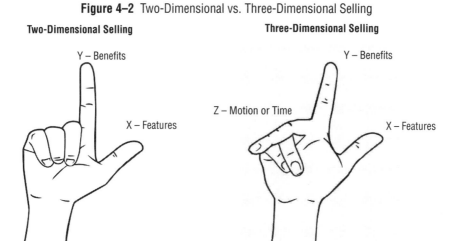

So, with BTL buyers, you are selling features and benefits, a two-dimensional model. With the ATL executive, however, you need to discuss features and benefits, of course, but also, and *most important*, you need to show how the product or service will benefit them *over time*—the last three to six months or the next three to six months. The questions you ask any executive should always be in the three-dimensional space of present, past, and future—and make past and future the real focus. In other words, you must Time-Travel your ATL with your questions, and not stay in that two-dimensional "fix it today" world of just features and benefits.

THREE-DIMENSIONAL QUESTIONS/COMMENTS

"What has happened over the last few months that is causing you to look at a solution this year?"

"What are the things you are looking for from this solution over the next six months?"

"Of the list of requirements you said you really need, which ones will be the most important as you roll this out over the balance of the year?"

"The demonstration today will focus on what you would use the system for right now, and as your needs change over the next six to twelve months."

There should always be motion in the questions you ask the ATL buyer. They live in a three-dimensional world. Yes, they operate in the present, but they are always talking about, going to meetings about, and making decisions about the last few months or the next few months. ATL execs are always Time-Traveling, and your questions to the ATL executive should reflect this motion.

You could ask:

"Mr. Hart, what are the initiatives in the next three months that are taking too much of your time?"

"What challenges have you been working on in the last six months that you need to stop working on?"

"Between now and the end of the year, what are the challenges you are facing that seem to take up the majority of your time?"

If you are looking for a key differentiator between selling below the line and selling above the line, it's the ability to ask three-dimensional questions. I've never seen an ATL jump on a salesperson's questions faster than when they concern the past or future.

Conversely, I've seen too many salespeople not have rapport with an ATL exec because they were living in today.

Master this line of questioning, even in your pre-call prep, and watch how you will get energy from the ATL buyer.

CHAPTER 5

Understanding ATL Energy

A sale is driven more than by just needs. For instance, many salespeople are concerned about their prospect's "sense of urgency." They can tell when a sale has that urgency, or energy. It's important since without it, deals tend to run out of energy, or get put on the back shelf.

Energy in a sale largely comes from the ATL exec. Now that you have understood a bit about the ATL buyer, let's tap into selling to them. As you can imagine, using BTL messaging and presentation materials is not going to work on the ATL executive, and definitely not work to get you the energy you're going to need to engage the prospect's sense of urgency.

CAPTURING THE ENERGY OF A SALE

Aristotle described pain and pleasure as very much a push-pull concept: human beings will move toward something that causes pleasure and will move away from something that causes pain.

British philosopher Jeremy Bentham said, "Nature has placed mankind under the governance of two sovereign masters, *pain* and *pleasure*."

Sigmund Freud stated, "We are born with a *pleasure principle*, that we will seek immediate gratification of needs, for which our bodies reward us with feelings of pleasure. The reverse is also true, and the *pain principle* says that, whilst seeking pleasure people will also seek to avoid pain."

The pain/pleasure theory says there are two things that motivate people—the avoidance of pain and the obtaining of pleasure; of the two, pain is a greater motivator than pleasure.

Understanding the Two Types of Energy

I place the questions salespeople should ask buyers into two categories:

▶ AWAY questions—those that focus on avoiding pain.

▶ TOWARD questions—those that result in pleasure.

When you are asking casual questions of the ATL buyer, you should start with AWAY questions first. Why? Because 80 percent of the people in the world, and ATL buyers, are AWAY motivated. Since that's a high percentage, it's safe to say that AWAY motivation causes energy.

AWAY energy is what motivates most buyers to change:

▶ We have to stop losing money.

▶ We need to minimize the time it takes to get this done.

▶ John needs to mitigate the risk on this new product launch.

▶ Mary will not make her numbers this year unless she stops discounting so early in the sale.

Although buyers are more responsive to AWAY reasons, TOWARD reasons can also hold sway:

▶ We have to make more money.

▶ We need to maximize the time we have to get this done.

▶ John needs to increase the risk on this new product launch if we are going to make the numbers we need.

▶ Mary will make her number this year if she just can take advantage of our pricing.

What will cause an ATL buyer to take some action, change what they are doing today, and actually get them off the couch? A problem. And with 80 percent of the world most strongly motivated by AWAY energy, it's safe to say that focusing on avoiding the pain of the problem is a sure way to intersect with the energy of the buyer.

ATL buyers will have one or more problems they are trying to solve, and if you can help in solving their identified top-of-stack problem, or offer some progress in getting closer to solving their problem, you are tapping into the ATL value proposition.

> A standard question in Silicon Valley when a startup wants to get seed money is, "Are you going to be an aspirin, or a vitamin?"
>
> Aspirins get funded; they solve a problem. Vitamins don't; they are nice to have but are not critical to the funder's success.

Other typical things an ATL buyer wants is to allay, alleviate, assuage, attenuate, blunt, bring to an end, a stop, a halt, or a close, close down, curtail, cut down or cut short, dampen, deactivate, deaden, decrease, dilute, diminish, discontinue, dull, ease, end, finish, interrupt, keep at or to a minimum, lessen, make less or smaller, minimize, mitigate, moderate, nip in the bud, prune, reduce, shut down, slash, soften, terminate, tone down, or weaken *their pain*. (AWAY)

So why do most of your voice mails and emails say you will help them to augment, build up, climb, enlarge, escalate, expand, extend, heighten, improve, increase, inflate, intensify, magnify, maximize, multiply, raise, rocket, shoot up, soar, spread, strengthen, stretch, supplement, surge, swell, top up, or upgrade *their pleasure*? (TOWARD)

Remember, only 20 percent of buyers are trying to move *toward* something; play the odds and go with the other 80 percent.

Okay, you now really get the difference between AWAY and TOWARD energy. We can move on.

I want to introduce you to a new mantra:

CSP—Customers Solve Problems

No problem, no cause; no cause, no energy. Pretty simple, isn't it? Of course, it should be a problem that affects their:

- Initiatives
- Fire drills
- Competitive threats
- Goals
- Challenges
- MBOs

Problems are what ATL execs are focused on, so if you can make a big dent in the problems they are working on or are trying to get rid of, you'll capture the ATL value proposition. Rarely will you be the total answer, for some of these problems are large. In most cases, you just have to be part of the answer.

FRAMING THE VALUE PROPOSITION DISCUSSION

To the BTL: We are the solution. It's what we are quoting in our proposal.

To the ATL: We can help you get closer to the change you need. You have a big and complex problem, and we can be a piece of the overall solution.

It's like you're the quarterback of the sale, and your job is to make a dent in one or more of the ATL priorities. In American football, the quarterback is the person in charge of the offense. He is usually the most visible and most highly paid position on the team. The job of the quarterback is similar to a salesperson selling ATL. The quarterback's job is not to throw passes, score touchdowns, read defenses, or take snaps. Those are tasks he must do to do his job. The job of the quarterback is to "move the chains."

In football, the field is 100 yards long and is divided into ten-yard increments. You have four plays to gain ten yards to get a new set of four plays, a new "first down." A pair of poles measures the ten-yard increments with a chain between them measuring exactly ten yards. If a team can move the ball forward ten yards within four plays, they have successfully "moved the chains" and have earned another set of four downs to go another ten yards.

The closer you get to the end of the 100 yards (the opponent's end zone), the better opportunity you have to score touchdowns or field goals. The job of the quarterback is to "move the chains"—to get the team in a position to have the best chance of scoring.

Your job as an ATL-conscious salesperson is to have the exec understand that the solution you are offering can make a dent, have an impact, or "move the chains" on their current problems and challenges—that your solution can help them accomplish their objectives.

Figure 5–1 The Roller Coaster

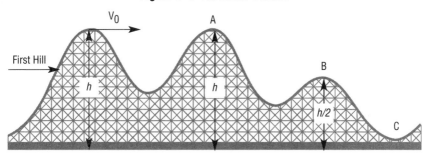

Access the Energy Early, Then Ride the Roller Coaster

For a roller coaster to be successful and get over that first big hill, it needs to gather energy: It needs momentum. It acquires that momentum by shooting you out like a cannon at the very beginning. The physics may be a little daunting (see Figure 5–1), but the principle is pretty clear: A deal, like a rollercoaster, starts with energy!

It's the same for a successful ATL sale. If you want to get a decision for your proposal in a timely manner, you have to have enough energy early in the process, and that energy needs to be quantified.

Quantify the Cause

Since the ATL buyer is an executive and executives always justify their investments, it's safe to assume that most, if not all, cause is quantifiable, that is, you can put a number to it. Number of dollars, number of units, number of market share, or even a number attached to a key performance goal.

"Unless we trip over our own feet, this project is worth $10M to us this year alone."

"The delay in getting those parts will cost us two months of production, which comes out to $5M."

"If we can't get this new product out by September, we'll miss the holiday shopping season and probably $3 to $5M in sales."

Not only does the ATL buyer know the size of the initiative or problem, they also can figure out what your solution does to their problem.

ATL executives know numbers inside and out. They know the size of the initiative or problem, and they can guesstimate what your solution will do for that problem and attach a number to it. For you to be effective, you *must get numbers* . . . period.

Think ATL When You're Thinking ASP or AOS

ATL executives know the size of the problem, so they can have a direct influence on the size of your solution. ATL buyers have a major influence on the average sales price (ASP) or average order size (AOS) of a deal.

If the ATL buyer is not involved early in the process, they will give the BTL buyer a budget (by the way, *budget* is a BTL word; more on this when we talk about vocabularies in Chapter 15). What the BTL buyer wants to do with that budget is up to them, but they better not exceed that number. Note that the User Buyer's budget lacks your input.

However, if you get to the ATL buyer earlier and demonstrate that you can "move the chains" on their initiatives or problems so the ROI is worthy of additional budget, they will find the money. Finding the money means an increase in your sales price, or a lower discount for the BTL.

HARNESS THE ENERGY IN ATL EVENTS

There usually is something that causes the ATL to start the roller-coaster journey—something that makes an executive get out of their chair and proclaim, "OK, that's it. We have to do something about this, and we have to do it now."

There are numerous types of events or situations that get the attention of ATL execs.

Boiling Point Events

Something has happened over time, and it just keeps building up until finally it needs to be taken care of, it hits a boiling point.

▶ A sales quota problem has gone on for too long, and the latest numbers show a worsening trend.

▶ A new product that just hit its thousandth complaint in the first two months.

▶ Results from a distributor show three times the normal sales, but they're going to drop you if you can't supply them with more product.

These are examples of nagging, lingering issues; emerging challenges; and problems that finally have had a match struck under them and the ATL executive has hit 212 degrees, and is going to do something about it.

Reactive Response Events

Sometimes things happen and there is no choice. Sometimes something happens fast—a competitor wins a major deal away from you, a key employee quits, a disruptive product comes into the market for 50 percent less than what you currently charge. Rarely can such events be planned for.

Change Events

A change event is a planned event and one that does not come on as fast as those that stimulate a reactive response, but it has to be dealt with. Change events usually sort out into some key areas.

▶ *Personnel:* Someone is retiring, reorganization is coming, a new department head is being announced.

▶ *Market:* A new channel of distribution is opening up, results aren't where they are supposed to be, or demand is shifting.

▶ *Competition:* New features, new customer requests, new competitors, or old competitors with a new product.

Timing Events

Good examples of timing events are a major trade show, the approach of a high selling season, or a competitor's announcement that they are going public and thus will get a lot of publicity.

ATL buyers have many initiatives and problems, and there is no quick fix for any of them. They have to be the quarterback—select the changes they have to make to achieve the maximum impact on their most important initiatives and problems.

Let's say a Chief Marketing Officer has this list of his top five initiatives for the year:

▶ Launch a new product by June 1.

▶ Define a new customer base and get 5 percent revenue growth by the end of the year.

▶ Add a channel of distribution that will be 10 percent of overall sales in eighteen months.

▶ Create new collateral for the sales team that will attract 10 percent more business for product line B.

▶ Create a new marketing campaign for a current product line that will cause overall sales to increase 2 percent.

Investments must be made so each of these initiatives can succeed. A salesperson who has a solution that will "move the chains" on one or more of these items will have ATL value and the ATL buyer's attention. Move the chains on some important initiatives or problems, and watch how fast an ATL buyer can respond.

There is, of course, that rule again about causes and problems; they must be quantified. You need to get numbers with cause. This makes a difference to the ATL exec, since usually they are his numbers. And it makes a difference in how you sell in a given ATL situation.

Look at the difference between what does happen and what should happen when you ask about goals and initiatives. The answers you get might include:

▶ We need to get more customers by the end of the quarter, or we will not make our plan.

▶ We have a huge customer churn issue; we have to do something now to stop the bleeding.

▶ Without additional funding, we won't have enough to finish the project.

The answers you *need* to get are:

▶ We need to increase our customer base by 10 percent by the end of the quarter, or we will not make our plan.

▶ With a 25 percent customer churn, we have to do something now to stop the bleeding; we need to get it down to 10 percent by the end of the year.

▶ Without another $100,000, we won't have enough to finish the project.

The objective and subjective nature of these two sets of statements is a double-edged sword. Subjective words describe passion, which can be mistaken for energy. They sound good too, and feel great to hear: *huge, a key, a ton, top-selling . . .*

On the other side of the sword, if you don't know the ATL numbers, don't expect execs to understand the numbers in your proposal. You can't prove ROI on words like *more, huge, a ton, additional, key, ASAP,* and *important.* ATL execs always talk in numbers, which is why you need to quantify the problem or cause.

A PERSONAL ATL EVENT

The battle for the remote is always fun.

As in my home, whoever has the remote controls the TV. One night, I'm watching something, but SportsCenter is coming on soon.

The couch I'm lying on is pretty comfortable, and SportsCenter is on the same station I'm watching now, which I'm really not paying attention to, since what I want to watch is ten minutes away.

In walks one of my daughters, with the body language and look in her eye that she wants to plop down somewhere and chill. I see her scanning the room, looking for the remote.

If she gets it, we are going to be watching something involving a Kardashian or a bachelorette, neither of which are on my radar. But, remember, the rule in our house is whoever has the remote rules.

You want to know what caused me to leap off the couch and secure the remote? What gave me a turbo boost of energy? It was the avoidance of pain—definitely an ATL event.

OTHER ATL ODDITIES

There are a few other things worth knowing about the world of the ATL exec. They are not really rules, but definitely hints that will help.

ASP and Speed—Increase the Velocity of the Sale

Another benefit in going to the ATL exec earlier is speed. A deal usually takes a shorter amount of time if the ATL exec is involved early. This is because:

▶ The ATL buyer wants to start getting the ROI as soon as possible.

▶ She has a problem and needs to show some progress on it.

▶ There are more critical items he wants his staff to spend time on; he wants this problem off their desks so he can start assigning new tasks that will effect new initiatives.

▶ Like a kid in a candy store, now that it has her attention and can contribute to the alleviation of a past or future pain, she wants it now.

There's a wealth of other reasons ATL buyers like to speed up deals. Knowing all the reasons isn't important. Just know that they *can* speed them up—and often do.

One Sure Constant: The Ongoing Need to Reassess Priorities

Priorities change all the time, and they usually change at the ATL level. Such changes are commonplace in many different areas, including:

▶ The competitive landscape

▶ Inventory availability

▶ Competitive pressures

▶ Market swings

▶ Key employees leaving

▶ A company's product mix

▶ Corporate reorganization

▶ Customer demand changes

▶ Economic changes

▶ Political changes

These kinds of changes usually happen from the top down, and you really don't want to spend a lot of time on presentations, demonstrations, and proposals while the organization is reassessing its priorities. That would be a lot of wasted resources on your part while "the news" is filtering down to the BTL buyer level, where the sales process generally starts.

The Buyer's Calendar

The ATL buyer's calendar can also have an effect on a sale.

Senior executives whose corporate calendar is the same as their fiscal calendar operate on quarters that can help predict their actions. Businesses are pretty predictable in terms of what is top of mind for them, depending on which quarter it is.

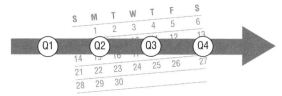

In the first quarter, ATL executives are launching new initiatives—some strong, others less so. If you are selling something that can have an effect on one of the newly launched initiatives that they are not feeling all that strong about, watch how fast a deal can move through the funnel. The logic here is all about the 80/20/80 rule.

ATL execs feel good on about 80 percent of initiatives they started the year off with, but it's that 20 percent of goals that are not going as planned that are causing 80 percent of the headaches. Help them identify and fix those 20 percent.

In the second quarter, decisions are being made on what initiatives to invest in and which ones to kill. These decisions need to be made by the end of this quarter, so management can attack the second half of the year in full stride.

The end of Q2 divides the initiatives into winners and losers. Those that are going well will get extra resources and extra attention; these are the ones that are going to make the company's year. They will get additional funding from the initiatives that are going to be scaled down or canceled.

Winning initiatives get more resources and more funding, which has to be spent fast—in the next few weeks and months—if the new resources are going to have any effect on this year's results.

By the time the third quarter rolls around, the focus is on getting ready to make last-minute adjustments for end-of-year success. The gaps for the year are being identified, and the execs have started to think about what needs to happen, what projects to ramp up, what things can be done to make the year a success—and ensure their bonuses.

In the fourth quarter, there are two objectives:

1. Make the number for the year. Do whatever it takes so the exec team can make their bonus.

2. Get ready to launch the next year, and not waste the entire month of January doing so and thus falling behind.

When you start aligning your sales advances to the ATL buyer's calendar, your probability of success increases greatly, since you will be aligned with the buyer's window.

BUYER'S WINDOW

Buyers can only handle what's in front of them, what is important to them at the moment. They can only do so much, so they prioritize. If what you are selling happens to coincide with one of the priorities that is being worked on, the buyer's window is open. If the buyer's window is closed, that doesn't mean they are not interested; it just means not now.

CHANGE IS KING

One way to summarize the various ideas presented in this chapter is that the real issue for ATL buyers is they constantly have to change things up. The business world is always changing, and if the execs don't change, they don't take risks. If they don't take risks, no decisions will be made, and they will soon be out of business or, at the very least, out of a job.

Find out what changes ATL execs are making, and why. What is causing (there is that word again) this change? You'll be surprised at how the ATL buyer will want to talk to you about their changes, especially when you have something that could help "move the chains" on some of their problems.

CHAPTER 6

Controlling the Inbound Sale

Sales are made every day. It's interesting to see what starts a sale. Is it customer demand, brand pull, market push?

From a salesperson's perspective, a sale starts with a lead. This lead can be *inbound* (the prospect is contacting the sales team) or *outbound* (the sales team is prospecting). The energy and amount of effort spent on getting a lead depends in part on where the lead comes from.

Figure 6–1, the Lead Energy Matrix, shows what needs to happen for an initial lead to be one that a salesperson should spend time on.

This chapter discusses inbound leads; outbound leads are discussed in the next chapter.

Figure 6–1 Lead Energy Matrix

	BTL	ATL
Inbound	Find out need. Qualify/disqualify. Get to ATL.	Ask about changes. Initiatives/problems. Find out cause.
Outbound	Establish need. Find out if budgeted. Get ATL.	Identify challenges. Time-Travel. Quantify.

The sales rep who intends to control the sale needs to take control right up front, starting with qualifying the lead. Too often, salespeople feel lucky to get a lead and use the energy from the lead to gather "hope" . . . hope that if they spend enough time with the lead, it will generate business. That is not the best use of a salesperson's time, obviously.

INBOUND QUALIFYING MADE EASY

Inbound leads require a different degree of qualification skills than outbound leads. Inbound leads can come from many sources, such as:

- ▶ A website hit
- ▶ A download request
- ▶ A mass email or mailing
- ▶ Names and contacts generated at a trade show
- ▶ Request for a trial
- ▶ Response to a marketing campaign
- ▶ Capturing attendees at a Web event

Anyone or any company knocking at your door is considered an inbound lead. Since there are numerous reasons prospects would knock at your door, a high proportion of these leads will be disqualified as "tire-kickers"—students, hobbyists, and people just doing random searches.

Many companies will score these leads and pass along only qualified leads to the sales team, or to a sales lead development team or rep. If a specialized team isn't doing your qualifying for you, the first thing you need to do is to qualify and/or disqualify an inbound lead.

LEAD SCORING

Lead scoring ranks leads to determine their sale-readiness. Leads are scored based on:

- ▶ The interest they show in your products or services.
- ▶ Where in the sales/buy cycle they are.

▶ How they fit ideal customer criteria assembled from current prospect/customer research

Leads can be scored using points—rankings like A, B, C, D, and F, or temperature gauges like hot, warm, and cold. Or they can be assigned weighted averages and then scored above a certain number—if they score above a 50, the salesperson should do this; above a 60, do that; and so on.

The most accurate lead-scoring models include both explicit and implicit information:

▶ Explicit scores are based on information provided by or about the prospect, company size, industry segment, job title, or geographic location.

▶ Implicit scores are derived from monitoring prospect behavior; they can include website visits, white paper downloads, email opens, and click-throughs.

Social scoring assesses leads based on relevancy and analysis of a prospect's activity on social networks and how much activity they are involved with on the Web.

Whatever the lead-scoring model used, getting high-quality inbound leads to the sales team is important and will help in sales productivity.

The Lead Energy Matrix says that when a lead comes in on the BTL level, your goal is to:

▶ Find the need.

▶ Qualify or disqualify the prospect.

▶ Then try to get to the ATL buyer as soon as you can.

Let's examine each one of these.

FIND THE NEED WITH THE THREE LEVELS OF WHY

The need is why the person is contacting you. They want to do something different than what they are doing today, and therefore they have a need. It could be something as simple as they woke up with a headache and need an aspirin, or their car was just stolen and they need a replacement, or anything in between.

To find out the true need, we developed a tool we call the Three Levels of Why.

Find the True Need

Three Levels of Why is a questioning technique that all good salespeople need to master. It is a way for the salesperson to understand the prospect's *true* need, both ATL and BTL.

People make a decision for a reason. There is a reason you wear the shirt you wear, drive the car you drive, live where you live. There is a *real* reason. But people don't like to talk about their real reasons, so they rationalize their decisions. And people don't like to openly discuss their rationalizations, so they develop *rapport reasons* to tell others why they made the choices they made.

Rapport reasons are typically what salespeople get when they ask questions in a sales environment. They are simple answers that the listener can relate to (hence the word "rapport"). Good salespeople get down to the second level of why, the rationalizations. Great salespeople know to go deeper and drill down to the third level of why to uncover the *real* reason. Here's a personal example of Three Levels of Why:

I just bought a new big-screen television for our family room. Why did I make that purchase?

Why #1: I wanted a bigger and newer TV.

Why #2: The 3-D movie features and the ability to download Netflix and AppleTV movies was compelling, let alone the ability to connect with the Internet.

Why #3: My wife had just finished remodeling the family room, and the new area where I would sit and watch TV is about two feet farther back than before. I now could not read the scrolling headlines or the posted scores on the bottom of the screen while watching SportsCenter. I had to squint, which would mean that I am starting to have a problem with my eyesight. Well, with the new TV, a 65-inch beauty, there are no more problems reading the small print, and I can still pretend that my eyesight is just as good as it was twenty years ago (LOL).

If you were the TV salesperson, you now have a real chance with me, since you know what's lurking at that third level of why. Show me a TV that allows me to see even the smallest things clearly while watching from a good distance, and you've got a sale.

Don't talk about the USB jacks, the remote, or even how a curved screen is the latest, coolest thing. Go after the third level of why, tap into my energy, and the sale is yours.

How do you know when you are at the third level of why? You know. Nonverbal signs, passion, voice inflection. How do you get there? You ask:

▶ Why: *"Why would you do that?"*

▶ What: *"What would that mean to you?"*

After the why and the what, flip it around and tell them what you just heard. Don't use their exact words, of course, but a careful paraphrase will let them know you've really been listening carefully.

▶ Flip: *"So I think I heard you say . . . , is that correct?"*

THREE LEVELS OF WHY: GETTING TO THE TRUE STORY

It never ceases to amaze me on how many Three Levels of Why stories people tell me. We introduced this tool over fifteen years ago in the first edition of *ProActive Selling*, and its popularity continues today. In the initial questioning of a lead it really does help to get at the actual reason that lies behind their motivation. We just ran across another Three Levels of Why story that really illustrates the concept.

We had a meeting with a VP of Sales who wanted some sales training for his people. When asked why, he said, "We need our people sharper. In our business they have to be quick at qualification skills and close the order fast."

When we drilled down into these issues, the VP said, "We are behind on the numbers and are having a tough time filling headcount, and the quota isn't getting any smaller, so while we are trying to hire more people, we need to make the ones we have smarter."

A lofty and passionate goal for sure, but with a little more questioning, here's what he finally said:

"We have 50 percent sales churn in our sales team. Not only can't we hire fast enough, but we are having a tough time replacing the ones we lose. If we can't stop the outflow of reps, we'll never catch up."

(continues on next page)

> So I asked, "So what you want to do is placate the salespeople so they stay, and you really aren't interested in making them smarter?"
>
> He smiled at me and we talked some more—but about their real issue rather than a window-dressing sales training effort.

Three Levels of Why is a tool to be used when you are asking a prospect questions about why they are making a decision, especially why they would buy from you.

We said above that you'll know when you get to the third level of why because the emotion, the passion comes out. Emotion fuels the third level, the true reason, and we maintain that most if not all decisions are emotional, and then they are rationalized, and then rapport answers are created. If this is true, the inverse must be true, and a salesperson must master the Three Levels of Why to get to the real reason and get a head start on qualifying the prospect. The emotional reasons a prospect would make a decision to start a sales process with you is what you really want to find out.

Left-Field Words

There are words a prospect uses that just seem to come out of left field, that seem to appear with no context.

Left-field words can appear when you are talking to a prospect, and you can tell the word has passion and depth to it, since it's just a bit out of place.

> "*I like fine* timepieces." (Most people call them watches.)
>
> "*That's an* unusual *shirt you have on.*" (Most people wouldn't call a shirt unusual.)
>
> "*Your solution seems to be a bit* dark." (Never heard of a solution being dark before.)

These left-field words, when you hear them, are great to use as you navigate the Three Levels of Why on your way to the true motivation, the real level of why.

QUALIFY AND DISQUALIFY

There probably are very few more important abilities for a salesperson to master than qualification and disqualification skills.

Qualify: The questions you ask and the things you do to keep a sales deal in the funnel.

Disqualify: The questions you ask and the things you do to get a sales deal out of the funnel.

On an inbound lead, qualifying and disqualifying are critical. Way too much time is wasted on deals that will be going nowhere, due to a lack of budget, energy, and focus.

There are many qualification methods out there, and they all are useful: IBM's BANT, *ProActive Selling*'s MMM, and Inside Sales.com's ANUM, to name just a few. To qualify a deal to stay in the funnel, you divide the lead up into three categories.

1. *Company Information.* This is information you will get that is particular to the company's product and services, and how they match those of a target prospect—its size, annual revenue, number of employees, etc., but really whatever information you deem necessary to keep a prospect in the funnel. There does not really need to be a "perfect" match, but a range of what is inside the norm should be defined.

2. *Action Information.* This is information you gather about their behaviors. Did they sign up for a white paper or a Web event? How many times have they hit the website? Have they talked to you before? What does their LinkedIn profile look like?

3. *Urgency.* How hot is this inquiry? Is there something they need to take action on now? This is always an important one and a tough one to really get right. Finding out if they have an I-Date (implementation date) is usually a good way of finding out if they are really interested in taking some action. So is asking about cause, which will tell you about their motivation.

Outside of not answering the qualification questions to your satisfaction, there are a few ways to proactively try to disqualify a deal from moving forward. You will want to answer the following questions before moving a prospect further along the sales funnel:

1. *Is there a true fit or a lack of mutual value?* The number-one reason salespeople do not disqualify a deal out of the funnel is the sense of loss. They will be left with nothing, and heck, something's better than nothing. You have to really provide a good fit and create value for the prospect, and they need to see how you can provide value. Forcing a bad-fit prospect into the funnel because of a lack of prospects or bad lead flow isn't a reason for passing a deal on to the next step.

2. *What is the Give/Get ratio?* The Quid Pro Quo (QPQ) method is always a good test to see if the prospect really wants to get involved, even if it's just to see if they can highlight two or three areas out of a ten-question email probing what is really important to them. Having them do something, anything, to put some sweat equity into the process at least shows they are willing to contribute and are not just window shopping.

3. *How broad and deep is the issue?* Asking the prospect about the problem, and who else in the organization this is affecting. Most prospects are looking at you because they are trying to solve a problem. Have them describe the problem, and then have them tell you others in their department or other departments that are being affected by the problem. How they describe a solution that would help them will demonstrate whether or not this is a well-thought-out situation, and the prospect is just not tire-kicking or gathering information for a hobby.

If you have decided that the prospect is truly qualified, the guidelines that follow should help you get control of the sales process.

GETTING CONTROL, STARTING WITH THE WELCOME

Control starts with the first contact. You can take a whole range of approaches, from the default "this is a prospect and the good ones don't come along often, and hey, they called us so it has to be a prospect" (not good) to really listening and asking questions to make sure you gain control early and stay there (good).

How to take the first step? There really isn't a "right" approach, but you can adopt, morph, or cut and paste some of the following approaches.

Here to Help

"How can I help you?" This is the classic first line, and if you're not careful, it's a great way for the prospect to gain control of the sale. If you do take this approach:

▶ Listen to what they say.

▶ Confirm what they have said (flip).

▶ Offer next steps—with rules.

Need to Register

This approach offers the prospect a classic Give/Get. They are coming to you because they want something; a white paper, a chat session, a free trial, an invite to a Web event. A requirement to register is a great way to start the call; the prospect gives something and you get something. Use their initial motivation to start the Give/Get process. You can do this in two parts:

Part 1—"I need your name, email address, title, and your sense of urgency on a scale of one to ten."

Part 2—"I'll be sending this to you." "This" is a key to unlock a trial, a link to download a white paper, or a free sample or one-time offer

Way too often, the need to register is passive. You need to be a bit more ProActive, and don't worry about prospects disqualifying out. It's okay . . . they were just going to take your time and eventually ruin your forecast accuracy anyway.

Offer Something "Special"

In negotiation terms, it's called nibbling.

▶ "Did you want french fries with that hamburger?"

▶ "If you buy two, you get the third one at 75 percent off."

▶ "If you stay four nights, you get the fifth night free."

Most inbound leads are BTL, so nibbling away at them with an hour of free technical support, or the ability to watch a demo video that is not offered to the public, or letting them sign up to help beta a new product is always effective in getting more information. People want to feel they are special, they are significant, and this is one way to do it, while doing a good job at prospecting.

Needs to Be Well Thought Out

Whatever your goals are for inside sales qualification, you need to consider the following:

▶ Is your lead flow one where you can afford to be selective, or do you have such a low lead flow that you need to open the valves to full?

▶ Can you get the name or the contact information of the ATL buyer?

▶ What information is going to be passed to the sales team, and is it consistent? Regardless of where the lead comes from, when it is passed to the salesperson, is there a standard format?

▶ How do you keep a disqualified lead available for possible future contact?

Getting Them Used to You

The goals of inside qualification efforts are many, but the driving goal is to get the prospect to feel comfortable. Get them used to talking to you. Let them feel comfortable as you take control of this sales call. This is not a control-freak thing; it's all about letting the customer make a decision to proceed or not. It's about controlling the sales process and letting the prospect see all the options in the way they should be seen, before they make a decision.

Build Rapport and Next Steps

Building rapport is a talent that can be learned. How you build rapport is important, and the sooner you build rapport with the prospect, the better. First, there are a few things you can do to make sure you are in a good position to build rapport.

1. *Put a mirror in your cube.* It will make you smile, give you feedback on how you are coming across to the client, and keep you on your toes.

2. *Write down the initial notes and the person's name.* There is so much going on in the first few seconds of the call that you need a roadmap. When you write down the prospect's name, get the spelling and pronunciation correct. Listen and write down at least two reasons they are contacting you, and repeat them back to the prospect. Use a cheat sheet and take good notes. People like it when they feel they have been heard, and getting all the details right and reading them back to the prospect gives you a chance to start to take control of this sale.

To keep the rapport going, you should be prepared with:

▶ Analogies.

▶ Very short stories of others who have been calling in who are similar to them.

▶ Humor—again keep any funny anecdotes or jokes short and sweet.

▶ Some Time-Travel questions that let the prospect talk about what brought him or her to you.

▶ Use the prospect's name often.

▶ Ask them to teach you something; people like to be a teacher.

▶ Compliment them.

▶ Paraphrase what they have said to make sure they feel understood.

There's a much shorter list of behaviors to avoid.

Avoid these behaviors at all costs:

▶ Talking about yourself   ▶ Interrupting them

▶ Finishing their thoughts   ▶ Telling your story after they tell their story

The first few minutes of the call are important, and if you are at your best, you can start to take control of the sale.

Countering Prospects' Stress

It's amazing how people stress out over contacting someone. When a prospect initiates the contact, their stress level is probably high. They may feel they are going to have to answer a ton of questions before you give them anything. Let them know you are glad they called (smile into that mirror in your cubicle—they will hear it over the phone). Speak in a calm and warm voice. Use your rapport-building skills to make them feel comfortable, *then* you can proceed to the next steps.

Cause Is Energy

If you remember one thing, it should be the word *cause*. Cause will lead you to the energy, motion, and strength of the ATL prospect, even at this early stage.

No ATL executive will take action without a reason, a cause. Top down or bottom up, ATL executives are reactive and ProActive, based on a change. Find out what caused that change, and you can judge how important the change really is. How many resources is the ATL exec or company throwing at it? A lot? There's energy.

Measure the energy the company is allocating to the change, and you can measure the energy—the resources, effort, and money—the company is going to expend on this change/initiative/problem.

CHAPTER *7*

Controlling the Outbound Sale

We learned a lot about qualifying the inbound sale in the last chapter. Now we move to the more difficult prospect—developing outbound techniques.

Outbound calling, also called prospecting, is something that has been around for ages. With the increasing use of technology, there are more and more ways to get outbound prospecting to work for you. Much less frustrating than trying to talk your way past some exec's admin or drumming your heels in reception, hoping to get a quick minute. Time to see what outbound techniques you can acquire for an ATL or BTL sale.

MAKE OUTBOUND
QUALIFYING WORK FOR YOU

An outbound lead is one in which the salesperson finds an opportunity. This can be done via either cold or warm calling.

Cold calling (also called *door knocking*) is calling into a prospective company when there is no established level of understanding or knowledge. Cold calling is not a very good way to get leads in most situations.

Warm calling is calling into a prospective company when you have a referral, a known entity, or some other valuable piece of information you can use to start a business conversation.

Typically, warm calling a lead is the preferred way to prospect. There are many different ways to warm call an outbound prospect. Tools that can be effectively used are:

▶ *Customer referrals.* A referral will get you in the door faster than almost anything. The prospect will call you back because they trust the person who gave you the referral. If they don't call you back, they probably aren't as good a friend as the referring person thought. Set yourself a weekly goal to obtain anywhere from two to ten referrals; networking will provide a constant flow of leads.

▶ *Online social tools like LinkedIn, XING, and Google+.* LinkedIn and its spinoffs have become a go-to for sales prospecting. LinkedIn is designed to become more effective the more you use it. Give recommendations, respond to requests, and see who has viewed your profile over the last few months.

▶ *Thank-you notes.* Brief notes to customers you just closed are a great source of leads. The VP of the company you just sold is really happy with you, and you should use that excitement to get a referral. Write an email similar to the one shown here, and ask new customers to forward it. They will be happy to do this, since they are excited, it will make them look good, and they have made a decision on something that they have and their friends don't.

Template for a Thank-You Note

Mr. Jim Smith

CXO

ABC Company

Dear Mr. Smith:

Just a quick note to say thank you for implementing the leading XXXXXXXX on the planet, and if there is anything you need or if you have any questions, please feel free to reach out to me. It's been a pleasure to work with the ABC Company team.

Additionally, if you know of anyone who could use our solution, or is having similar business issues that you had before you implemented XXXXX, would you please just forward this e-mail on to them?

Really would appreciate the opportunity to help some other people/companies that you know.

Thanks again,

Skip

P.S. If Jim sent you this, I can be reached at skip@m3learning.com.Thx!

YOUR HOMEWORK

For an outbound prospecting effort, the level of homework you need to do is dependent on a number of factors, especially the following:

▶ Quantity of lead flow

▶ Quality of leads

▶ Average sales price

▶ Number of large opportunities available

Homework is a great way for you to get up to speed and not just spew information. Really be interested. Bring your natural curiosity to the table; really try to understand where the prospect is coming from and what they do. This is a much better attitude than doing homework on a company with the idea of selling them something right away. You can break homework into three levels.

Level 1: A Quick Look-See (Baby Bear)

For most leads, a quick look is more than adequate. For a lead where you have just a name and a company, you should start by looking at the company's website to get a general picture of who they are and what they do. Then you will want to look at some basic financial information to make a quick temperature check:

▶ What is their annual revenue?

▶ What is their revenue growth over last year?

▶ How are their profits compared to a year ago?

▶ What are they forecasting their year to be and how does that compare to the previous year?

Then go on LinkedIn and find the person:

- Do you have a connection with the person?
- Do any of your connections know the person?
- Who is that person connected to?
- Where did the person work before, and do you have any contacts there?
- Find something in common, if possible—a mutual contact, a previous company, or something about where they lived that you can relate to.

After this quick look, you are ready to make contact.

Level 2: More In-Depth (Mama Bear)

For this level, you do Level 1 stuff, but add the following:

- Look at the leadership of the company, including the officers, the board of directors, and advisory boards.
- Read the first page of the last annual report.
- Compare last year's financials to this year's, looking at revenue, expenses, and total assets.
- Compare their financials quarter by quarter, not just year by year.

Financials can tell you a lot. For example:

- If revenue is up by 10 percent year over year, and expenses are up 20 percent, the company is investing in something or has made some bad choices.
- If revenue is flat, and total assets, including cash, have gone down, the company is spending money on something, hoping to get revenue growth.
- If revenue is up by 20 percent and expenses are up by 10 percent, the company has money to spend on future growth somewhere.

And by the way, if you don't know how to read financials, you might want to make it your business to learn how (sorry, more homework).

Spend an extra few minutes on the company website, look at more detailed financials, and maybe Google some of the analysts' comments.

If it's not a public company and you cannot get financials, Google the company and try to get at least the number of employees and number of locations. Search some local papers for the company name and see what they have made the news for. Any information is better than no information.

Level 3: Real Homework (Papa Bear)

If you really think this prospect is worth it, dig in, especially if the lead promises to be an ATL lead, or if you know or sense that this account can be a potential whale for you. (*Whale* is a Las Vegas term for "big spender." In sales, it means a potential huge account.)

In addition to the research you've done on the two levels above, do the following:

▶ On LinkedIn, check out all the corporate executives who might be interested in your product/service.

▶ Look at current 10K report on their website.

▶ Get stock information for the past twenty-six weeks.

▶ Listen to the audio version of the last financial analyst's report. Listen to the whole thing, if you can. If not, the first and last ten minutes of the call are usually very interesting, especially the analyst's questions to the management team who are on the podcast.

Homework is an important part of prospecting. Remember: Your goal is to keep the focus on them. It will definitely keep you from pitching.

GETTING PAST THE SCREEN

There is quite a lot of advice out there on how to get past a screen, and getting into this subject in any great depth would require another book. Short of that, some tips include:

▶ Try befriending the screener, rather than going over their head. If you talk in ATL language, you'll separate yourself from most prospecting calls, and if you try to enlist the help of the screener, they may even try to help you.

▶ Keep it all about them.

▶ Pose questions that assume the screen has behind-the-scenes knowledge: "Have you heard your boss say something like . . ."

My book *Knock Your Socks Off Prospecting* has more information on this topic if you really need it. (And there are other good books out there.)

GET TO THE POINT—
THE ONE THAT'S ALL ABOUT THEM

When you're prospecting and selling ATL, the time from interest to no interest can be faster than the speed of light. Here are five rules to follow:

1. It's all about them. If you mention who you are or what you do more than once, they are not going to listen.

2. Short, short, and shorter.

3. Affirm and don't interrupt, especially with your stories.

4. Engage in some Time-Travel by asking "back in time" or "forward in time" questions.

5. Insert energy or urgency when you can by posing AWAY questions and asking about cause.

One of the most important things when you are making ATL calls is to have an idea of what you want the outcome or the next step to be. What do you want the prospect to do and what does the prospect want you to do? This is not the time for you to be doing all the doing.

"That's great, Mr. Smith. As a next step, why don't I get a fifteen-minute presentation ready for you to see? How's next Thursday?" (Bad)

The above approach is bad because you have left the prospect with nothing to do between now and next Thursday. Is the prospect supposed to be sitting around and waiting? You have to give them some homework. The next step needs to be mutual, not you doing everything. Insert some energy by giving them something to do.

"That's great, Mr. Smith. As a next step, why don't I get a fifteen-minute presentation ready for you to see next Thursday? I'll send you a sample

agenda tomorrow, and if you could highlight the key areas that you want to cover and send it back to me, I'll make sure we cover what's of real interest to you." (Good)

And this approach is good, because the exec is part of the action.

THE PROSPECT'S HOMEWORK

If you want to get someone involved with something, have them take a first step. Homework assignments are a part of the transfer of ownership and qualification arenas. You want the ATL prospect doing something while you are preparing for the next meeting.

You don't want them just waiting for you to get back to them. If they have no homework to do, then by the time the meeting is a day or so away, since they have no skin in the game but are just going to listen to you talk, there's a high probability of you getting bumped for another meeting. Only some "sweat equity" will motivate them to see that nothing gets in the way of the next meeting.

ATL execs are always willing to accept a homework assignment. They know if both parties are involved, the better the meeting will be, especially if the homework assignment focuses on them and is in their best interest.

A list of typical homework assignments can include small individual work assignments that can take a matter of seconds (mini-homework) and larger ones that will require some work (real homework).

Mini-Homework

Lightweight homework assignments might include asking the prospect to:

▶ Review and prioritize the agenda the day before the meeting.

▶ Have them send a copy of your email to someone else in the organization and cc you on it.

▶ Acknowledge a personal invitation sent by your manager. (For example: "Hello Mr. Smith, I'm Charlie's (the salesperson) boss, and I'd like to invite you to a one-on-one talk, an executive overview, a private showing . . . Please respond . . . ")

▶ Review your understanding of the sequence of the sales process events, with a request for confirmation or correction.

▶ Prepare an executive briefing.

▶ Fill out a pre-on-site visit questionnaire.

▶ Review the specifications.

▶ Give a preview of a promised hall walk-around.

▶ Quote options: what you will be expected to provide.

▶ Review I-Dates mentioned in earlier conversations.

Real Homework

More meaningful homework expands the engagement of the ATL buyers in the sales process. Some suggestions follow:

▶ Ask for detailed goals of the project.

▶ Ask for the ROI on the initiative.

▶ Ask for initiatives this effort will affect the most/first.

▶ Request past examples of successful projects implemented.

▶ Probe for expectations for the first thirty- to ninety-day results.

▶ What other business initiatives might benefit if this investment exceeds expectations?

If you don't ask for involvement, then the ATL exec's interest will diminish. Getting more of their time will be hard.

ATL execs want to put some effort into the sale. They know they are not going to get something for nothing. If it is going to move the chains on some initiatives, then what's a little homework?

If you believe a salesperson's job is to do what the customer tells you to do—that if you do what they ask you to do, and you do it well, you will get the order—you are seriously mistaken. It's time to change your thinking.

GIVES/GETS

Early on in an ATL sales effort, you need to establish a quid-pro-quo relationship. The best way to do this is to come up with a set of Gives/Gets.

For everything you are going to do for an ATL exec, you should get something in return. Without this mutual relationship, chances are you are going to be treated like a vendor and not a partner.

A Get is a homework assignment you can ask from the prospect to make sure they have an interest in this process. Send them an email with the five topics being talked about in the meeting on Thursday, ask them to circle their top two or so, so you can be as prepared as possible to maximize the time they are spending. If they aren't willing to take a few seconds to maximize an hour or so of their time, then you should consider stopping the sales process, since the energy for this deal at the ATL level is probably pretty low.

Examples of Gives (your input) and Gets (the ATL homework assignment) are:

Give	Get
Initial presentation	Validation of agenda for next meeting
Pre-education call	Provide company background information
Education presentation	Background of attendees and interests
Demonstration	Sample data
Detailed proposal	Red-lined markup of rough draft
Final proposal	ATL exec in attendance

Use these homework assignments, and think of some other ones, to allow for transfer of ownership of the solution one step at a time and to disqualify unlikely prospects as quickly as you can. Make lists of potential homework assignments and Gets and keep them near your phone so you always have them available to you; otherwise, your "wanting to please" sales mentality may overpower your "wanting to give them a homework assignment" mentality, which would not be good.

The ATL value proposition is different than the BTL value proposition. By getting the ATL information you need early, you will set yourself up for two value propositions at the end of the sale, get faster decisions, and block out a lot of competitive noise.

CHAPTER *8*

Stage 1: Being ProActive

Stage 1 is kicked off with the buyer's initial interest.

From an ATL exec perspective, Stage 1 begins with an ATL event—whatever is causing them to change, to "get off the couch" as it were, and apply energy to a situation. Let's assume you will have to be prospecting to these executives, since it's rare that they call you and proclaim, "I'd like to buy something now!"

PROSPECTING TO THE ATL LEVEL— STRATEGY AND TACTICS

Getting to an ATL exec is not all that hard. What's hard is getting their attention and then *keeping* that attention so they will give you more than five minutes of their time. Let's start with the homework you need to do before the call.

Understanding Executive Personas

We covered the three levels of basic homework (Baby Bear, Mama Bear, and Papa Bear) in Chapter 7. In addition to the basic information about the person and the company that you learn, what also should help you build rapport at each executive level is understanding what each ATL function does, their *executive persona*, if you will. There are a great many executives in the C-suite, and more titles are appearing all the time. (Everyone wants to be a chief something.)

We discuss the major executive functions in broad strokes below. As you read, develop a list of questions around each executive persona, since a Chief Financial Officer (CFO) at one company usually has the same problems that the CFO has at another company. There will be common threads that can form a framework for the questions you'll ask them when prospecting at the ATL level.

Chief Executive Officer (CEO): A CEO has three main duties. First, he or she sets the vision and strategy for the entire company: making sure all operating functions, projects, and plans contribute to that strategy and meet the assigned and agreed-to goals. Second, CEOs set and drive the culture of the company. Culture is always top down. Third, the CEO is the company leader and key spokesperson. All employees take their lead from the CEO, and being ProActive and positive is a key part of the job.

Chief Information Officer (CIO): The CIO wears many hats as he or she runs the computer systems for the company and makes sure the company's technology links with its strategy. CIOs are also the gate-keepers for changes to the technology; good ones know how to say yes as well as no. Most CIO organizations serve all the other C-levels and all lines of business users, so they need to balance the needs of all departments. They also contribute to the overall competitiveness of the business, including revenue generation by selecting and sup-porting IT programs that affect revenue, like e-commerce initiatives, marketing automation tools, and CRMs.

Chief Operations Officer (COO): Often known as VP of Operations or Director of Operations, the COO directs functioning of the com-pany, and its policies and production goals. Where the CEO is in charge for setting the vision and the strategy, the COO makes sure everything is running right so the company ends the year where they want to be.

Chief Marketing Officer (CMO)/Chief Revenue Officer (CRO): The CMO is responsible for the overall strategy and budget of the company's marketing plan, including internal and external branding initiatives, advertising strategies, and channel marketing. He or she is also responsible for the overall performance of the marketing department. The CRO is usually the VP of Sales, with inside, field, and channel sales and revenue responsibility.

VP of Engineering and VP of Manufacturing: These executives oversee new product development, usually with input from the CMO.

Chief Financial Officer (CFO): CFOs are responsible for the financial well-being of the company. They oversee financial operations and provide guidance in budgeting, forecasting, business planning, accounting operations, and procedures. The financial voice of the company, the CFO is usually strategically involved with projects that include initiatives for revenue growth or cost-cutting.

Office Manager: Surprised to find this BTL manager in a discussion of the C-Suite? Well, this individual is important when you are selling ATL. Known as the Office Manager, Executive Assistant, or Executive Manager, this BTL manager speaks fluent ATL. Any given exec might have one. They typically help the ATL executive do their job, but they are much more than a glorified secretary or assistant. They know and influence schedules, and at times provide intuitive advice. Not respecting this position is a mistake many salespeople make. Make sure you develop rapport with these people.

If your product or service focuses on one or two of the titles described above, you probably should spend some time researching what those executive personas typically do and how they do it.

Research their company records by quarter. Also do general searches like "What is on the mind of a CFO for second quarter 2015" and see what comes up. Having an up-to-the-minute understanding of what key ATL executives do will help build that all-important rapport you will need when you finally get to talk to them.

MASTERING THE ART OF THE SHORT EMAIL

The goal of an email to the ATL suite is to grab attention and create some energy. Typically, you want your email to generate a response; you want it to make someone want to get in touch with you or be open to your next step—for example, a phone conversation or an in-person contact).

Emails That Work

Mr. Jim Smith

CXO

ABC Company

Dear Mr. Smith:

Very quickly, I'm Skip Miller with XYZ Company. CXOs have been recently asking us:

- How can I get a head start on my mid-20XX objectives and avoid potential cost and resource gaps?

- What are the new competitive risks that I need to be aware of?

- How can I optimize my processes without an increase in budgets?

The rest of 20XX is starting to look optimistic on many fronts. Can you spare 15 minutes so we can talk tabout your challenges and gaps for the rest of this year to see if there is a financial reason for us to get together?

Regards,

Skip

*   *   *

Dear Mr. Goodman,

Very quickly, I'm Skip Miller with ABC Company. Regarding the rest of 20XX, I'd like to discuss with you a couple of points related to your company.

When would you be available for a 10-minute call?

Thanks,

Skip Miller

*   *   *

Dear Mr. Goodman,

Reaching out to you, since over the last few weeks, we have been hearing questions like these from CXOs:

- "How can I mitigate the risk of losing critical data, clients, and financials?"
- "Are my teams relying on tools that are actually slowing the growth of my company?"
- "What are CXOs doing to reduce operational expenses now?"

I'd like to share with you some ideas and see if there is a reason for us to discuss.

May I call you on Monday, November 12? Could you please provide a telephone number?

Thank you,

Skip Miller

These are very simple, to the point, and "all about them" emails. Save your pitch for later if you need to. You are just trying to get their attention.

Subject Lines That Work

Good subject lines are important. An easy reminder is RAN.

▶ *Relevant*—Make the subject line relevant to the executive persona, the industry, a current topic, the time of the year, or an important trend.

▶ *Address concerns/problems*—Everyone has problems, but you should be able to guess what is keeping this executive persona awake at night. Some diligent research will yield a list of concerns and problems you can use in a subject line.

▶ *Name*—Not *your* name! The name of a mutual friend, someone the exec works with or who works for them, someone in their industry they would know, or one of your more popular customers, by name or company name. This name needs to be someone you know as well.

Here are some examples of subject lines that will motivate ATL execs to read your email:

▶ Jim Koll suggested I get in touch with you

▶ Quick question about Q2 revenue goals

▶ Clarification on quarterly objectives that Mary mentioned

▶ 10 months to go and behind targets?

▶ Your product XXX rollout challenges

A subject line must be very short. It should be just enough to make them want to take that first step: clicking it open. Remember the following when writing emails and subject lines: Make it fit on a smartphone! According to data from the *US Consumer Device Preference Report*, 65 percent of all emails in the United States are now being accessed via mobile devices—and that number will only increase.

Make sure the executive you're targeting can easily open your email on a mobile device and not have to scroll too much to read the subject line and message.

Using Email to Get a Referral

Email can be an easy way to arrange a referral.

Hi, John,

Hope you're doing well. Do you mind introducing me to Trudy Baker? I would like to discuss with her a couple of points related to XXXXX and potential collaboration with my company.

If you prefer not to, no problem -- just let me know.

Thanks for your help.

Best,

Skip

Have someone you know forward your email to the person you want to contact, which they can easily do when they reply to you.

Introducing Yourself via Email

If you need to introduce yourself in an email, the rule is the shorter the better—and make it about them.

Dear Ms. Jesse,

I would like to introduce myself as your Account Manager here at XXX Solutions, Inc. We work with companies in your industry, like ABC, CDF, and XYZ, to:

- Reduce IT management overheads and licensing costs
- Provide tools that reduce communication/collaboration friction
- Improve the scalability of the business to easily pivot to varying market conditions

I'm going to call you in a few weeks to introduce myself, and see if there is a reason to discuss these types of issues further.

Regards,

Skip Miller

XXX Solutions, Inc.

Trial Intro

The email that follows is a good one, since your questions are paraphrasing what the prospect is probably asking themselves, and the postscript has been personalized.

Hi Ms. Jones,

I tried to get in touch with you regarding your trial with XXXX but could not reach you. When someone like you requests a trial, they usually have questions like:

- How can I get a quick look without wasting a lot of time?

- What is the best way to see what it can do without getting lost?

- Is there a way to see 80% of what I need to see in 20% of the time?

Please let me know if I can answer these or others. I'm here to help.

Regards,

Skip

P.S. Attached is a link to a video on how to get started. It's about 15 minutes, but if you go to 3:12 on the timer and watch for about 3 minutes, you should get a quick understanding.

HOW TO LEAVE A PHONE MESSAGE

There are two types of voice mail messages to leave. When properly designed, both can help you get what you want: a face-to-face conversation with the ATL exec.

Request for Help

You dial the number and hear, "Please leave a message at the tone, and I'll get back to you as soon as I can. *Beep.*" Here's what you say:

> *"Hello, Mr. Falls, my name is Jason House from the ABC Company, and I could really use your help. Please call me back at 909-123-7890."*

The components of the "I need your help" speech are:

▶ *Introduction:* State your name and your company—no more, no less. You do need to state your company's name, since otherwise the prospect will be left wondering who you are.

▶ *Call for help:* Keep it simple—you are just asking for help. Don't give a reason why, just ask for it. You will be surprised at how many ATL execs want to help.

▶ *Request action.* Let the prospect know where to call you back.

Here's why this works:

1. There are many people who want to help if your request is sincere.
2. You are keeping to the script, and not talking about you.
3. You are honest, you really can use their help.
4. It's a legitimate call. When the prospect calls you back, just ask for directions.

When the call is returned, the conversation might go like this:

"Hello, Jason? This is Ken Falls returning your call."

"Yes, Mr. Falls, thanks for the callback. The reason I called is that my company, XXX, helps other companies reduce the burden of travel expenses and travel reporting. I could use your help in determining who in your organization would be responsible for looking into something like this."

It's a legitimate call. You are asking for directions (whom should I contact?). You can save this company a ton of money, and if they have been looking into an issue like this, they probably should be working with a vendor like you. If they aren't looking at this issue, they probably should be. It's all about their ATL value proposition. If they were looking at something you could contribute to, why wouldn't they look at you?

How can something so simple be effective? We have consistently documented over the years that salespeople who use the help request have a callback rate of more than 30 percent. Why? Because people generally want to help.

An addition to this speech is based on a referral. But be sure to use the name only of someone who will help you to build rapport. Now when you hear, "Please leave a message at the tone, and I'll get back to you as soon as I can. *Beep.*" you say:

"Hello, Mr. Falls, my name is Jason House from the ABC Company. I was talking to Deb Davis, and I could really use your help. Please call me back at 909-123-7890."

And, of course, Deb needs to truly be someone you know and someone they know. It could be a referral, a coworker, or someone prominent in the industry. Don't lie. Don't say, "I was talking to the president of your company" or something that your prospect can easily check out.

20-Second Pattern-Interrupt Speech

What pattern are you trying to interrupt? The one in which the prospect identifies your call as a sales call and presses the delete button. In this instance, when you hear the beep, you say:

> *"Hello, Ms. Lane, my name is Kurt Leaf from the ABC Company, a leader in the offset printing market.*
>
> *"The purpose of my call is that I'm talking to a lot of VPs of Manufacturing right now, and I'm getting questions like: 'How can I increase production without increasing costs?' and 'How can I get faster delivery times than I'm getting today so I don't fall behind schedule because of lack of ink?'*
>
> *"If these are some of the questions you are thinking about as you look at the next few months, please give me a call at 909-123-4567 so we can discuss your potential options."*

The 20-Second Pattern-Interrupt Speech breaks down into:

1. *Introduction:* State your name and one feature of who you are or what your company does. This will take three or four seconds, just enough time for the prospect to decide she's heard enough and is going to make a judgment call and delete this message. At this point, you want to break the pattern.

2. *Pattern Interrupt:* The prospect is probably going to delete your message right about now, so this is where you break the flow.

   > *"The purpose of my call . . ."* (Purpose . . . like what?)
   >
   > *"The reason for my call . . ."* (OK, get to the reason . . .)
   >
   > *"Why I'm calling . . ."* (OK, why? I'll give you a few more seconds.)

It's like when you're sitting in a lecture, which is interesting but not interesting enough to keep you from getting mighty sleepy after fifteen or twenty minutes. Then the speaker says, *"and in conclusion . . ."*

"and in summary . . ."

"and finally . . ."

That wakes you up. It interrupts the pattern of the speech. Usually after a pattern interrupt you listen more intently. So use the words *reason, why, purpose,* or anything else you can think of at the three- to four-second mark to break the usual voice mail pattern.

3.   *Questions:* Nothing transfers ownership and gets someone thinking like questions. Use two here so you're not depending on just one roll of the dice.

These two speeches—the Request for Help and the 20-Second Pattern-Interrupt—will get your prospect to call you back. It's a great way to start you off on the route to a face-to-face sales call.

Voice Mail Essentials

We leave voice mails all the time, but smart salespeople do the following when they're trying to set up a meeting in the C-suite:

1.   Get to the purpose as quickly as you can. Say the word *purpose.*

2.   State your name and company up front.

3.   Be sure your name is absolutely clear. A major reason people do not return voice mails is they don't hear who is calling. Speak slowly throughout your whole message, and enunciate carefully. Record yourself and listen to how you leave messages, then ask yourself, "Would I return this call?"

4.   If it's possible you are not going to be around to take the return call, keep your voice mail greeting short and to the point.

> *"This is Sam Waters. Please leave your name and number and I'll return your call as soon as I can."*

5.   Be positive in your tone. Make sure you're smiling, because that comes through over the phone. No one wants to respond to a robotic or depressing message.

TRUMPETING

If you really want to do a complete job of ATL prospecting, try trumpeting. When you develop a lead, either outbound or inbound, before you contact the BTL user, send an email or social media message to the half dozen top officers in the company.

Dear XXXX,

I just received an inquiry from your company. We plan on following up on this, and if there is a financial reason or a real issue that can be impacted, I'll send you some more information. Thanks in advance.

Regards,

Skip Miller

Account Manager—XYZ Company

An outbound lead would be similar.

Dear XXXX,

Based on your website and some current financial data, there may be a financial reason or a real issue that can be addressed in a 15-minute discussion.

I'll send you some more information before I call so you can make an early decision. Thanks in advance.

Regards,

Skip Miller

Account Manager—XYZ Company

With this outbound trumpet, you can add a link. If it's a private company, you probably have no financials, but you can say "based on something I've read," "things I've seen in your industry," or statements to this effect. Let them know you have done some research on them, that this is not just a form letter.

You would not believe the hallway and back channel conversations that can go on after you send out these emails. You decide whether you want to send them out individually or all in one send that shows who is being copied. Additionally, if you want to include the BTL lead's name on the email, again that's up to you. Try some different spins.

▶ Have the letter come from your boss or even your president.

▶ Use some customer names to show they are in good company, but don't use their competitors as customers; ATL executives always want to be different.

▶ Tie it to an event, either yours or theirs.

▶ Use the Buyer's Calendar (see Chapter 5) to tie it to business events on a quarterly basis.

Most ATL executives want to be "kept informed." That's all you are doing here. You are letting them know that if the reason you are contacting them becomes important enough and ATL enough to need their attention, you'll let them know when you meet. It's a status update about an inquiry that was made of you, and what ATL exec doesn't want to have the status of something updated with them? It's also a great way to create noise (thus the moniker *trumpet*).

Trumpeting is another example of prospecting tools that work but most sales organizations don't try, because they prospect BTL too heavily and wouldn't dare go around the person who has made the initial contact, or go over the head of a past contact.

Well, it's your choice. Do you want to tap into two energy sources or one?

Let's end the chapter with that question (not that we don't know the answer by now). We've discussed a lot of ideas and techniques here. In my seminars and training sessions I've learned the value of a timely break, so—I'll meet you at the next chapter after lunch.

CHAPTER *9*

Basics Never Go Out of Style

Hey, good to have you back. Everyone full? Not too full, I hope (napping not appreciated).

More about being ProActive in the prospecting and qualifying stage. It never ceases to amaze me how salespeople, entry level to the most senior, have trouble with the openings to sales calls. They either blurt out too much information, try to think of something witty to say, or just wing it. Are these options good enough for a professional salesperson?

It's time for the outbound sales person to have a strategy on their intro phone calls. Time to reengage the 30-Second Speech.

START THE ATL PHONE CALL
WITH A 30-SECOND SPEECH

"If I can just get past the first few minutes, I'm okay. It's in that first minute or so that I have a tough time."

There are many, many salespeople who feel this way. There is no one best way to make sure the first few minutes of a phone call are always perfect, since a lot has to do with the person on the other end. Follow these guidelines to make the first few minutes of an ATL call less stressful.

After introducing yourself, you need to ask questions. Not enough to get the prospect annoyed, but a few questions about them, their business,

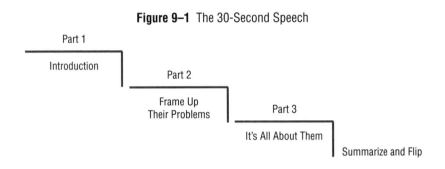

Figure 9–1 The 30-Second Speech

and the gaps they are trying to tighten up. A good outline for this is a 30-Second Speech broken into three parts and a conclusion (see Figure 9–1).

Part 1: The Introduction

This is where you introduce yourself and your company. Keep it simple and brief. "Hi, this is who I am, and this is my company."

"Hi, Mr. David, I'm Skip Miller with M3 Learning."

By the way, it's a bad idea to start the conversation with "Hey," "Dude," or "What's up?" but you already knew that, I'm sure. "Hi" and "Hello" are much safer bets; leave the slang at home when you are calling at the ATL level, even if it's "who you are."

The ATL exec is a busy person, with problems that need solving. They don't want to hear about you until they believe you are listening to *them*. Having them believe you can help them solve a problem or close a gap comes after they talk to you about their favorite subject—themselves and their issues.

They don't care about you; they care about themselves. Get through the first part of the introduction (who you are) quickly and easily. You'll have time during the in-person sales call to tell them more about you and your company if they are interested.

Part 2: Frame Up Their Problems

Now is the time to tell the prospect about you, but briefly. Keep the focus on what you help companies avoid, minimize, or stop doing (remember AWAY messaging, which is talking about problems).

"Quickly, what we do is allow companies to stop throwing money at risky decisions by giving them a visual analytical tool that executives can use at their desks, so they stop being hampered by IT reporting delays."

Simple AWAY messaging and making sure it is in motion or is action-centric is the best approach. In framing it up, many salespeople want to be boastful about who they are and what they offer, since they are proud of what they sell and the company they work for. While this is admirable, it's not going to get the attention of the prospect up front.

Part 3: It's All About Them

After you briefly frame it up for the prospect so they have some idea of what problems you can solve for them, you want to shift the discussion even more decidedly to them. You want to now interest the prospect in terms they can understand and get them interested enough to start a discussion so you can determine the appropriateness of a next step with this client.

> No executive or prospect will ever agree to meet with you because you have something to tell them. They don't care. They will agree to meet with you only because they have a question they need an answer to. Get the question out first. Getting the information in will come later.

For you to accomplish two key objectives—getting their interest and getting them involved with the conversation—Part 3 should be in a questioning format.

Questions get the prospect to think and take ownership. If they are good questions, which means ones relevant to the prospect's concerns, they will think:

"Yes, these are questions I ask myself all the time. Was this person at my last staff meeting?"

"Yes, these are some of my issues, and there are some other ones I really would like to have the answers to. This person is talking in language I can understand. Maybe they have some ideas."

"No, these are not the questions I ask myself, but they are close. Let's talk about it."

The prospect has to think and get involved when you are asking questions. Two questions you now should be asking yourself are:

1. "What are good and relevant questions?"

2. "What kinds of questions should I ask?"

The answer to what are good and relevant questions is easy. You have already done some homework on this prospect. Use it to formulate questions the prospect would be interested in.

The second question is even easier. Remember, *it's all about them.* Keep the conversation focused on them for the moment to build trust and rapport. What questions would the prospect be asking themselves as they sit in their chair?

CUSTOMER CHAIR QUESTIONS

"Is there a way to save time on my new product launch? It's already two months behind schedule."

"How can I increase revenue in the short term without getting additional resources?"

"What can I do to get my sales team selling this product without having to give additional commission for the rest of the year?"

Part 3 is for asking questions that stimulate the prospect's interest and get them involved. It's why they will allow you to talk with them, because they have questions.

Ask great questions to get their questions and issues out on the table and then start a dialogue, and it had better include questions the prospect is asking. It's not about mind reading; it's about perspective. The transition between Part 2 and Part 3 is called a "bridge." You have to create a bridge in between Parts 2 and 3 to transition to the questions. Bridge phrases can be:

"Executives like yourself are always asking us . . ."

"Companies we talk to are asking . . ."

"Major companies like yours are having questions like . . ."

"People in your position are always asking us . . ."

"Some homework I have done on your company shows you are probably having questions like. . ."

Go with whatever bridge phrase you feel comfortable with. It doesn't really matter which one you use; it matters that you have a bridge phrase that leads into questions in Part 3.

Summarize and Flip is how you end the speech. You summarize the questions you have asked, then flip the conversation back to them so the prospect starts talking.

"Mary, these are questions we are hearing from CMOs recently. . . . That said, what are the initiatives that you are focused on for the rest of the year?"

"John, these are questions that many CEOs are discussing with us. . . . As you look at the upcoming year, what are your top objectives and strategies?"

"Kalpit, these questions are things we are hearing a lot on the street recently. . . . As you look at your company over the next few months, what challenges do you see in the area of revenue growth?"

There you have it, the schematics of a good introductory 30-Second Speech. Some basic rules:

Rule #1: Don't just jump in with a 30-Second Speech. There usually are a few moments of idle conversation. Pace yourself. Examples of introductions are:

"Is this a good time for you?" (the permission call).

"Mr. Patel asked me to call you" (the reference call).

"I was doing some homework on your company and discovered there may be a reason . . ." (the homework call).

Whatever your style is, use what you feel comfortable with.

Rule #2: Have some fun with it. "Hello, Ms. Reynolds. What's your schedule look like for the next forty-five seconds?"

Rule #3: Email your 30-Second Speeches. Emailed 30-Second Speeches also work very well. Just be sure you keep the focus on them and remember to Summarize and Flip. However, the goal is not for you to seem scripted. Keep it simple. If you introduce yourself without too much fanfare, frame up their problems, and ask the prospect questions about themselves, you will be as successful. Period.

Rule #4: Sound like yourself, not like this book. Memorize the flow, not the exact words really, so you can be yourself. The more genuine you sound, the better you will be received.

THE ART OF ASKING QUESTIONS

The Law of Prospecting says an executive will agree to meet with you only because they have a question on their mind that they want to ask. It's up to you to ask questions to get the prospects' issues on the table so a discussion can take place that will be all about them. This is very, very important.

Sales management spends a lot of time training their salespeople in product knowledge so when they get in front of a prospect, usually a BTL User Buyer, they can spew out what they know. There are even names for this phenomena: Spray and Pray, Show up/Throw up, Crop-Dusting. Reactive salespeople spew product knowledge and do it with enthusiasm.

They have PowerPoint slide shows, PDFs, videos, and handouts, all in the name of "educating" the customer. All this is great. There will come a time where education is important, but good salespeople know that great questions are not just something they think of at the spur of the moment. They need to be practiced like anything else.

How to practice asking great questions? *Be the customer.*

When you are doing your homework, put yourself in the customer's chair. Even physically move if you have to. Ask yourself, "If I were the customer, what would be important to me as I look at the rest of the year? What is keeping me awake at night as I look at what I have been trying to get off my desk over the past few months and just can't get rid of?"

If you were the prospect, would you really be asking yourself, "How would I use this guy's product or service?" Heck, they don't even know about your product or service. They do not care at the moment. It's all about them. They are thinking about *their* problem, the thing that is causing them to do something different. They have to change what they are doing . . . but how?

Questions will win the day, and you need to have done your homework to really think, "What questions are on my prospect's mind?" Don't just do this planning in your mind. Write some questions down and have a discussion with your boss, with other salespeople, or even with current customers. Ask them the questions you are thinking about asking your prospects in order to add some depth to those questions.

Practicing questions will give you a leg up and stop you from executing the "All About Us" sales model (Spray and Pray) when you are on the call.

If you're still not convinced, here are seven reasons you want to master the art of asking questions.

Reason #1: Use questions to cause problem-solving motion. One of the most effective ways to approach any problem is to ask questions about it. The greatest thing about questions is that your brain automatically starts working on them as soon as you ask them. Not only that, but it'll keep working on them in the background, when you're not even aware of it.

Reason #2: Direct the sales call with questions. Good questions guide and direct the call. Think of them as your control knobs for the sales process. They can lead the prospect to discuss problems and challenges they are having and need some help on. Good questions help the prospect explore why they have to change and their fears or risks of that change.

Reason #3: Do what teachers and coaches do. Ownership takes place when students and athletes figure things out for themselves. Do you remember the best teacher or coach you've ever had? They are the ones who made you think, made you figure it out for yourself. Coaches don't hand a playbook to an athlete and say figure this out for yourself. They ask questions, just as teachers do of their students. Coaches and teaches who talk and talk, especially in those lecture halls, are not as effective as ones who ask questions.

"How can we run this play differently?"

"What do these last three pages mean? What is the author trying to say?"

"If there is one minute left in the game, how can we run this play?"

Reason #4: Questions shift attention to the prospect and his problems. Salespeople can be the two-dimensional, fix-it type of people we discussed in Chapter 4. Give them a problem and watch how fast they have a solution. It's what they get paid to do. Find a problem, solve it, get the order, cash the commission check.

When you turn the problem into a question, the two parties participate and work together to find a solution. Framing up problems and restating them as questions lets everyone participate and shifts everyone's attention—including the salesperson and their "I have to fix it now" mentality—to the problem at hand. Only then can the collaboration with the prospect begin.

Questions get everyone to take a more exploratory look at things, which gets everyone involved. Questions encourage creativity. Questions get prospects to talk about solutions they have tried, ones they have not tried, and ones that they would be open to. Sure beats sending them a proposal and then never hearing from them again.

Too many times during sales conversations the salesperson has an answer and wants to share it. There are many reasons for this, including the salesperson wanting to prove her value or move the sales cycle along. The brain is very analytical, and seeks answers for questions naturally. It wants answers, and when a salesperson has "an answer," watch how fast she cuts off the ATL prospect or at the least finishes his sentence. Bad, bad, bad idea!

When asking questions, remember the Three Levels of Why (see Chapter 6). If you stay focused on the prospect and get to the third level of why, you will avoid blurting out solutions; this allows the prospect to figure out the solution for themselves. (Remember our mantra from Chapter 5: "CSP — Customers Solve Problems"?)

Reason #5: Keep questions centered on the customer chair. Questions are powerful communication tools, and they are also great at simulating your prospect's thinking. Get into the mindset of your prospect. Play this questioning game with a few of your colleagues.

USE ROLE-PLAYING BEFORE THE ATL SALES CALL

Have a colleague sit in a chair facing you and assume the role of the VP of XXX at the prospect firm. Base your questions on what's on her mind at this very moment, considering:

▶ The Buyer's Calendar   ▶ The current marketplace

▶ Organizational issues   ▶ Limited resources issues

▶ The current demand for   ▶ Employee issues
   products like yours

Ask questions of this faux VP. The more questions you feel comfortable with, the easier your initial few minutes with the actual client will be.

Reason #6: Make questions part of how you look at things. A salesperson who asks great questions is usually the one at the top of the leaderboard. Great salespeople are not the ones with the best answers; they are the ones with the great questions—ones that are about the prospect's problems!

Have questioning become a part of your sales day, every day.

▶ Why is this prospect calling in?

▶ Why are they not making a decision? I should ask them. They are going to save money daily by implementing this. What is the problem?

▶ Why did they agree to the demonstration? What would be the outcomes they are looking for?

▶ How about that VP. She answered my email. Why did she make the effort? Does this mean she's really interested in our services?

The more you ask, the faster you get to a decision.

PARAPHRASING AND SUMMARIZING SKILLS

There are many ways to end the first few minutes of a call, as well as the call itself. Paraphrasing and summarizing are two good techniques—both serve to reframe the earlier part of the call.

Paraphrasing is designed to clarify the buyer's understanding. It is a question that lets you be very clear about what the prospect is saying, how they feel about it, and the importance they are placing on it.

You paraphrase when you want to check your belief about what has been said, want to make sure you have the facts as you have heard them, and want agreement from the prospect on your interpretation. You are checking in with the prospect, gaining agreement, and increasing rapport. The prospect is being heard; they feel they have been understood.

By paraphrasing the first few minutes, you will gain clarity from the prospect, and that will encourage you to forge ahead with the sales call, side by side with your prospect, instead of speaking *at* them. This can also be used when the initial conversation comes to a stall, and it seems like there is nowhere else to go. Paraphrase, then ask a Time-Traveling question such as, "So what would this mean to you over the next few months?"

Since you asked the question, you are the one in control.

A *summary* is an overview of the main points that you have covered in your ATL sales call. You summarize to make sure everyone is on the same page. Summarizing is different than paraphrasing, since paraphrasing is usually covering one or two thoughts, and summarizing is usually covering most or all of the meeting.

Follow these steps to master summarizing.

First, create a break with the words like, "Let's summarize what we have said, okay?" and start with what the prospect has said. Itemize in concise fashion the main points (three is a good number) the prospect has relayed to you.

"John, you have said that: one, you need to get revenue ramped up in 50 percent less time than it is taking now; two, the current method is not scalable; and three, you need something that will integrate with the current IT system. Is that right?"

Next, summarize what *you* have said. Keep this brief and focus on one or two key points.

"I've said we might have a solution that is worth having another discussion about, yes?"

Finally, gain agreement. Listen to and watch what they say and how they say it to uncover any "hidden objections." Make sure you have taken good notes, and don't just rely on your memory, since the words the prospect uses are just as important as what they have been saying.

TIME-TRAVELING

Chapter 4 had a major section on Time-Traveling. Suffice it to say that, on the opening sales call to an ATL exec, all questions, paraphrasing, and summarizing should incorporate Time-Travel. A two-dimensional question or statement can ruin the beginning part of a sales call. Always ask three-dimensional Time-Traveling questions.

"So what do you see as the biggest challenge between now and the end of the year?"

"What is the key area of the new product launch that has bugged you over the past few months *and caused you to call us?"*

"As you look at the next few quarters, *what will be the two or three things that may keep you from hitting your goals?"*

When you paraphrase, you want to Time-Travel as well.

"So it seems that as you look at the next couple of months, your inability to get the data you need in a timely manner may keep you from hitting your goals. Is that right?"

"What you are saying is that the current production capacity will not be able to meet demand in ninety days, and this will negatively affect next quarter's earnings. Yes?"

Of course, also engage in Time-Travel when you summarize.

"Mark, let's review what we have said. You said the next three months are going to be very difficult, and may affect 10 percent of this year's revenue.

You also said that if you don't get this fixed in the next thirty days or so, you might have to cut revenue estimates. I said we might have some answers for you that may include our new product offering. Is that about right?"

If you don't engage in Time-Travel with an ATL exec, you might as well not even have had the meeting. They Time-Travel all day long; in meeting after meeting, they exist in a world of three-dimensional time. Why would they want to address a two-dimensional question?

NEXT STEP

Finally, it's time . . . time for you to make a decision. The seller and the buyer have a choice of several courses of action, right?

1.   The buyer makes a purchase now.

2.   You ask to see the decision maker.

3.   You arrange to give them a demo.

4.   You give them a proposal.

Nah, don't think so. It's not time for any of the above. The most useful next step is to ask:

"Should we both continue in this process?"

You and the prospect get to decide. The next step should be a *buy step that requires a sales step along with it.* So the options are:

▶   An Education step that would include a sales presentation.

▶   A Validation step that may include a demonstration.

▶   A Justification step that may include a working proposal.

You both choose if you should continue with the process. Just make sure that you:

1.   Put the buyer's step first.

2.   Make sure there is something for them to do too.

3.   Stay in control.

You are never too old to go back to basics. That said, you need to have an introduction speech format you feel comfortable with. Practice this for a week or two. It will stop sounding rehearsed and will feel natural to you—and therefore to your audience.

When I do a 30-Second Speech, I half expect the prospect to stop me in midsentence and proclaim, "That's a 30-Second Speech!!"

It's never happened. Usually I hear, "Great summary of what we want to talk about today."

CHAPTER *10*

Sharpen Your Executive Business Acumen

Companies are predicable. Most have run the same way for years. There's a great sameness in their organizational structure, the products and services they provide, the employees they hire, the profits they make, and the shareholder value they deliver. And while some do it much better than others, in the long run there isn't much difference between Company A and Company B.

If you look at companies in a specific industry, you'll find close organizational similarities. A pharmaceutical company may be somewhat different from a gear manufacturer, but most pharmaceutical companies look similar to one another, and so do all the gear companies.

You use information about how companies run to improve your selling to ATL and BTL buyers. A company's goal is to make money for its stakeholders. That's never going to change. But from an operational view, how does a company work?

TOP DOWN AND BOTTOM UP

What drives a company is the old economics game of supply and demand. Make or buy something at one price, sell at another, and the difference is profit. It doesn't get much simpler than that.

In most companies, the organizational structure is built around this idea. You have a CEO or president who is responsible for the whole thing. Then you have departments that make the business work: manufacturing and engineering, to design and manufacture what is being sold; marketing, to develop the ideas and let the world know what you are doing; sales, to take the orders; and finance, to collect and manage the money.

Other functions are necessary to keep the company running: HR, to manage employee issues; IT, to keep the data processing and communications systems running; purchasing, to buy the stuff the company needs to make and sell.

Let's watch how a company runs to see opportunity. From both the bottom-up and top-down viewpoint, things at your company are running fine. Systems are in place, the products are being shipped out the door, and there are profits being made. All is well.

Then of course, something happens.

▶ A competitor enters the market and offers something very similar to your product at 30 percent less.

▶ A newly available system can manufacture the products you are making for 25 percent less, and most of that savings can go right to the bottom line.

▶ A new application for what you are selling will allow you to sell twice as much as you planned for. However, the systems you have now cannot work any faster, and you don't have enough employees to make, market, and sell into the new demand.

Pick one or all of the above. In all the scenarios, something has to change or profits will suffer, the company will make less money, and that will not make the owners of the company happy.

Change: The Great Motivator

The change that is coming will cause decisions to be made, very likely including new goals or objectives. These goals will pose challenges to company personnel since:

▶ What they are about to do, they have never really done before.

▶ It must be done quickly, since the company will be losing money: either because it costs too much to do it the way it is being done, or because they will be losing sales.

▶ There are risks in every decision they make, and since there are a lot of decisions, the less risk the company has to take on, the better.

The good news is that these changes create opportunity for the salesperson. Your job is to understand what the company is doing now, what it wants to do (its new goals), and how to help it get there. To see how, let's look at the Big Red Door Company.

Big Red Door Company

Let's use this example to figure out how to get the attention of the ATL and BTL buyers. This company makes big red doors.

President Kerry Porte runs BRD; he is second generation of the Porte family, which owns a majority of BRD.

The organizational structure is shown in Figure 10–1.

▶ Kerry Porte–President

▶ Jean Moss–Kerry's executive assistant

▶ Mark Hills–VP Engineering

▶ Sean Little–VP Manufacturing

▶ Amanda Li–VP Sales

▶ Susan Smith–VP Marketing, also known as CMO

▶ Alex Wright–CFO

▶ Doug Notes–VP Information Technology, or CIO

▶ Mary Green–VP Human Resources

The management team of BRD is doing well and getting ready to plan for the new year. There are a few things the team is considering.

▶ A new machine is available on the market that can make doors faster. Production can be ramped up 40 percent. Next year's goal will reflect this ability to make more doors than BRD is currently making.

Figure 10–1 Big Red Door Organization Chart

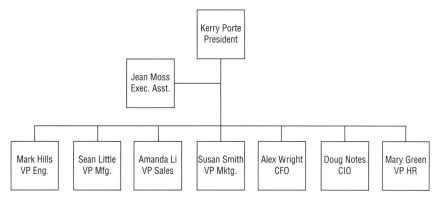

▶ BRD sells doors to the U.S. market through its U.S. sales team. The sales team will get its usual 10 percent annual increase in quota, but will also have to absorb some of the 40 percent increase in production, and will get a 5 percent increase in its budget, enough to hire three more sales reps. That's a 15 percent growth target at minimum for next year, not counting new product line potential.

▶ Marketing needs to help increase demand for the additional capacity and will get a 2 percent increase in its current budget to accomplish this.

▶ Since production can be ramped, marketing and engineering are working out a plan to add two new product lines.

All of these changes are based on the availability of the new door-making machine. Of course, with any new goals or initiatives there are some problems.

THINK ACROSS THE ENTIRE ORGANIZATION

If you look at this one change as just a change, you may not get a sale. If you look at how this change affects all the departments in BRD, you may find some opportunity.

▶ Engineering is under pressure to develop new door styles. They have an idea of what they want to do, but the marketing staff has only created initial designs for the kinds of doors that would be most in demand, and they have not done any customer feedback sessions.

▶ Manufacturing needs to have the new equipment up and running by the first of the year. The model they want is on backorder, but they can get the next model up for only $100,000 more. The CFO is looking at the risk of waiting vs. the cost of the more expensive model, and while everyone is examining the possibilities, the clock is ticking.

▶ IT has just reviewed the specifications of the new machine, and getting it online will require some major reprogramming. Also, loading the new parts in the old CRM system will require some additional time. If IT is going to focus its resources on this project, the new HR system will have to wait to be implemented at least six months.

▶ The president just came back from a major trade show, where he gave a keynote speech and basically announced the new products to the market. The problem with that is the people who saw the early designs were not that impressed, and Kerry thinks they need some work if the 15 percent increase for next year is to be attainable.

▶ The budget for the new machine as well as all other costs has been already allocated, and some of it has already been spent.

What is taking place for each member of the executive team based on this one change?

Kerry Porte has already committed the company to 15 percent growth, at a minimum. If BRD had not taken advantage of the new technology, its sales would have been flat at best; their production was near capacity, and because of a 10 percent growth in the market, they probably would have lost market share.

Mark Hills in engineering is ready to design the new doors, but one person quit a few weeks ago, and getting some dedicated time from someone else who can design the new doors is going to be tough. Also, there never has been a technology upgrade to the current design system, so it still takes twice as long as it should to get designs out.

Sean Little's manufacturing department is getting the new machine, and everyone wants to be a part of it. People still need to work on the old machines to hit their production targets. The training on the new machine will be critical to its success, and all five of the machine operators want to go to the training class, but who will run the current machines if everyone is out of the factory for a week?

Amanda Li in sales needs to hire three more salespeople. The problem is that finding them and bringing them up to speed could take six months minimum. That wouldn't put them on quota until midyear. How can sales make the new numbers in only half a year with three new hires?

Susan Smith in marketing sees that with the new products come a host of challenges. There is the need to go ask customers what they want, to work with engineering to finalize the designs. She also needs to launch new marketing programs, create new sales collateral and training, and, with sales, fine-tune forecasts by geographic area. This is all a lot of work, and she does not have anyone on her staff who has launched a new product before.

Alex Wright in finance sees that the 40 percent increase in production should give revenue a boost, but he didn't count on the machine being more expensive or on delays due to lack of availability. The new budgets have already been allocated and can't be changed.

Doug Notes in IT knows that since the new machine is not compatible with the current system, a new interface will have to be written and tested, while not messing up current processes and systems. With the limited resources currently in IT, other projects are going to have to take a back seat.

Mary Green wonders, with the possible delay in the new HR system, how can HR tie into the new databases of potential new hires and sort the candidates by expected success? Mary was counting on the new system being up and running by the first of the year, so she would be able to streamline the new-hire resume and application process the company is going to need. Without that system, getting a pool of qualified candidates is going to be hard.

Of course, Jean Moss probably has the most difficult job in the entire company, but isn't directly involved with the various challenges facing the C-level execs (although if you build rapport with her, it can do wonders for your access to them).

With the new goals come challenges, since no one has all the answers—and with these new challenges comes opportunity.

ATL AND BTL SOLUTION BOXES

Each department now has some problems they need fixed. Answers will be coming from the bottom up as well as from the top down—from below the line as well as above the line.

Let's look at Mark, the VP of Engineering. Mark has additional budget to get the new designs out. However, Jerry, the lead engineer, has been looking at a new CAD system that will save time in the design process. So Jerry's solution is to spend the $25K on a new CAD system. Let's call this Solution Box A.

Mark has a problem—to get the new designs ready for manufacturing by the first of the year. He knows he needs to do this better than the way he does it today. The new designs will bring in 10 percent more revenue to the company, but Mark sees a one-month delay in getting the designs out. That will cost the company about $200K. He has to close this $200K gap. Mark also needs a few other things to go right to help close this deficit; for example, he needs to hire a new design engineer. There is a rumor about possibly moving to a new facility. We'll call this Solution Box B.

For Jerry, you are the complete solution because you are a CAD salesperson. His entire Solution Box A is a CAD system. He has gotten approval from Mark to go look at systems, and has a $20K budget that is being talked about.

When, as a CAD salesperson, you call on the Big Red Door account BTL, you will be talking to Jerry about the features and functions of your product. Jerry will be excited and want a demo, a proposal, all the right things.

You will try to get to Mark, the C-level buyer, in order to give him an overview of your system, but you'll find out that Mark really doesn't care that much about it, since he has delegated that responsibility to Jerry.

From the bottom up, the BTL buyer wants a CAD system. From the top down, the ATL buyer has to get a new designer on board, get a CAD system (optional, in his view), and oh, possibly move into a new facility, all while trying to get a new design out one month quicker than normal so he can close the $200K gap he is responsible for.

A good salesperson will call on Jerry and make sure that what Jerry wants—the BTL features and benefits—Jerry gets. He will also call on Mark, and ask Mark about his challenges. Mark will talk about his Solution Box B, and he and Mark together will decide the CAD system can make a dent in the $200K gap (which it can, so watch Mark get Jerry the $25K he needs to buy the system).

However, if you want to speed up this process, you want to go hunting for Trains.

TALKING ABOUT TRAINS

Mark, being the engineering VP that he is, has numerous problems he needs solutions for (Solution Box B). Look at his problems:

▶ He has to get a new design out one month early and get a new hire on board—like, yesterday.

▶ He has to get the entire engineering department moved into the new facility in four months (looks like the rumor was true).

▶ He has to get the new upgrades to the current product line done in ninety days.

Let's call each one of these problems a Train, and Mark is the station master (Jerry is merely one of the conductors). You call on Mark and ask him what are his biggest challenges, and he tells you about Train 1, the new design.

Well, a CAD system would certainly help with that. You go right into how your system can speed up development, save time, and blah, blah, blah. Okay, you would help with one Train, but how about the other Trains Mark is facing. To play the metaphor out, he has to get these Trains out of the station so new Trains (challenges) can come in and be addressed.

The smart salesperson knows that if his solution can help multiple Trains, then there will be additional energy from the ATL buyer, and additional money and speed will be allocated.

The salesperson asks Mark what other challenges he faces before he launches into his formal presentation, and finds out about the upgrade to the current product line, which of course a CAD system could help with. So now, the salesperson has found at least two Trains that he can help Mark move, and now Mark is paying attention. There is more value to Mark now than there was when they were talking just about the new design.

Mark now sees this CAD system making a big dent, probably about half of the $200K problem. Additionally, he has just talked to Louise, the head of the design maintenance staff, and she believes if she had a CAD system, they could delay a new hire by six months, which would give Mark at least $50K of additional budget money he did not have five minutes ago, and that would more than pay for the $25K needed for this CAD system.

Mark is getting two of his Trains addressed—not completely, but he's making major inroads—by acquiring this CAD system. Demo? Not really needed for Mark, as long as Jerry and Louise are happy.

When hunting for Trains, you are going to take a top-down approach. Start with the ATL buyer, find out his Trains, and see how many you can address. Usually two to three is a good number.

When selling below the line, tread softly when hunting multiple Trains. Jerry, who is the conductor on Train 1, will usually not know too much about other Trains, and doesn't really want to share unless he has to anyway.

Train Station Rules

As with any tool, there are rules and guidelines you may want to pay attention to.

1. Every ATL executive has multiple Trains in her station, and the Trains are always changing based on when challenges get completed or are reassigned.

2. Trains differ in their importance. Some are "local" and some are "express." The express Trains are the ones with the most energy.

3. ATL station masters don't want to talk about your products/services . . . yet. They are paying their conductors to solve those individual problems.

4. They want to talk about their Trains, however, to anyone who will listen, since they have to get those Trains out of the station. They need to come up with answers; it's what they get paid the big bucks to do.

5. Station masters with C-level titles all seem to have similar Trains.

6. It's easier to build upon current Trains than invent new ones.

Keeping the Trains Running

Big Red Door is an example of top-down and bottom-up selling. Each of the executives of BRD had Trains they needed help on. The CAD system might have solved some cross-departmental Trains as well, like those linked with manufacturing and IT. It's a backward approach to present your solution to as many BTL types as you can in the hopes of hitting more than one Train.

It's much easier to go to ATL buyers and ask them about their Trains and gaps (gaps are discussed at length in Chapter 14), and then help them to be a part of the solution, if not the entire solution.

You are the entire solution for Solution Box A, belonging to Jerry, the BTL buyer. To Mark, the ATL buyer, you will make progress on two Trains in his Solution Box B. The CAD system just got funded and ordered at $25K.

Yes, this is an oversimplification, but, if you continue the BRD story and look at all the ATL executives, look at how much opportunity there is for a salesperson based on this one change.

Most large sales involve multiple Trains and multiple departments. Hunt for the challenges, then offer your solution as part of the total solution.

BECOME THE CHAMPION OF SOLUTION BOX B

Now that you have seen how Solution Boxes work, you should look at a sale from two points of view—an organization standpoint and a project standpoint.

Anytime you start attaching yourself to a project, you are probably going after Solution Box A, and the BTL buyer. When you attach your sale to a department or organization, it's probably Solution Box B.

Examples of Solution Box A:

▶ *"I have a budget of $20,000."*

▶ *"This will help me get my job done faster."*

▶ *"We need to send this out for a RFP."*

▶ *"We need to see a demo."*

Examples of Solution Box B:

▶ *"I need to save three months on this effort."*

▶ *"The risk to the company over the next few months could run upward of $500K."*

▶ *"If we get this, I can see two or three different projects this could help us on."*

▶ *"I'm losing money daily by not getting some answers."*

NOTE TO THE PERPLEXED READER

Yes, it would have been easier to have Solution Box A be for ATL, and Solution Box B be for BTL solutions. But Solution Boxes have been around for ten years, since *ProActive Selling* first came out, and you can't change history. However, if you want Solution Box A to stand for the ATL buyer, and Solution Box B to stand for the BTL user, go right ahead. It only matters that you keep them straight.

I-DATE FOR BOX B

Without taking anything away from the overall message, Implementation Dates (I-Dates) are key for both Solution Boxes. The BTL buyer wants to start doing something different now. The ATL buyer is losing money daily by not making a decision, and they want to make a decision, but only if it contributes to one of their Trains before it "leaves the station" (Solution Box B's I-Date).

An ATL exec with Trains in the station has an expected launch date (I-Date) for each Train, or a date when they need to get an issue off their plate, since when the initiative is ready to go, and most of the glitches have been solved, out of the station the Train goes.

If you can get to the right ATL buyer, try to get an I-Date for Solution Box B, not just the part you are addressing. You will find once you get an I-Date for Solution Box B Trains, you will be put on the fast track, and your sale will take a lot less time than previously predicted.

CHAPTER 11

Stage 2: Don't Forget The Split

There is quite a bit that has to happen in the beginning part of a sale—doing homework, qualifying and disqualifying a lead, understanding BTL and ATL outcomes. However, you are now past the first stage and are ready to go to Stage 2, where education happens, and so does The Split—the separation between what goes on above the line and below the line.

Once a lead has entered Stage 2, the overall goal is mutual education. A two-way education process has begun, in which the buyer really has to understand what the salesperson and his company is selling, and the salesperson and team has to understand what the real needs are of the prospect, now and into the future.

This two-way education process is very important, and its actions are scalable. We have seen some sales teams just gloss over this with a fifteen-minute conversation, while other teams spend a huge amount of time, most of it wasted. The general rule is the more time you get to know what your prospect's real need is, the better.

Here is the big *however*—at Stage 2, you have to honor The Split, illustrated in Figure 11–1 (yes indeed, sharp-eyed reader, you have seen this before, as Figure 2–4).

Let's look back at what we discussed in Chapter 3. The salesperson gets a lead and qualifies it, and the process goes forward to Stage 2.

Figure 11–1 The ATL–BTL Split

The Cause/Effect Split

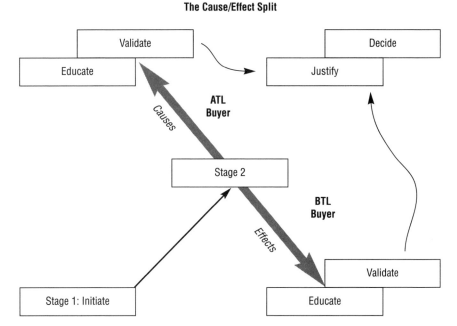

At Stage 2, the deal splits. There are now two value propositions, one ATL and one BTL. Salespeople know the BTL value proposition well—it's all about our product/service and what we do—and we are very comfortable with this discussion, so here's where we tend to hang out, below the line.

Below the line, we ask the question, "Okay, what are you looking for? What are your needs?"

The prospect responds, "I am looking for . . ." and then lists four or five key things they want the solution to do.

For example, they may say they want a solution that:

1. Is faster than the current system.

2. Is more flexible than the current system.

3. Will interface with the current system.

4. Will provide 24/7 support.

5. Comes in under $XX,XXX.

Figure 11–2 The Split—Separation

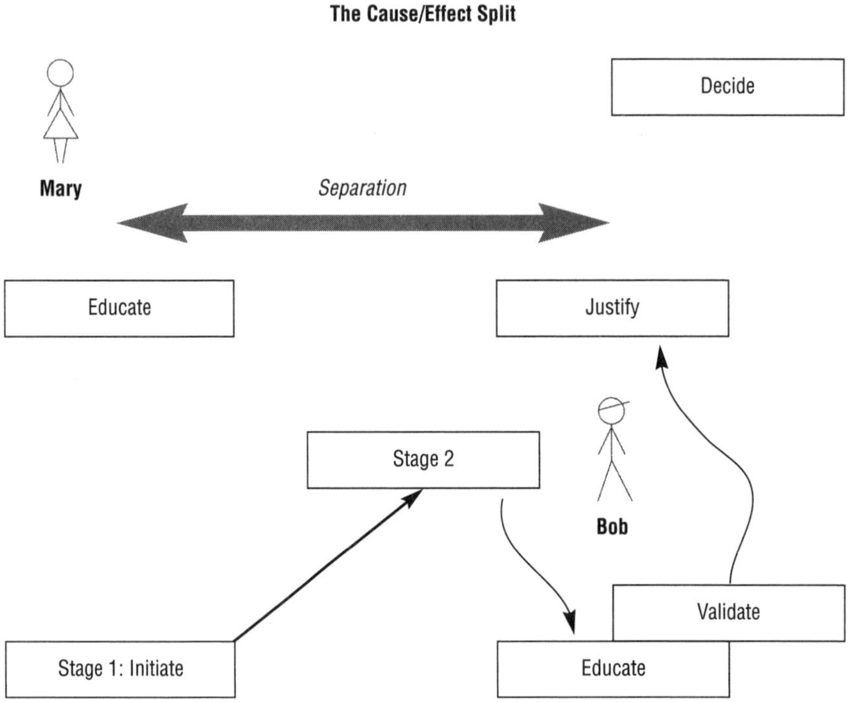

The Cause/Effect Split

When you hear this, you get really excited, since your solution does most or all of these things, the budget sounds tight but doable, and you can already see this sale in the bag. You take the next step, and offer an in-depth presentation of what you do, followed by a demonstration.

The demo went really well, so you start tossing numbers around, formalize a quote, and send a proposal to the prospect. Things are looking good. You can even start forecasting this to your manager. Your BTL buyer, Bob, has told you they expect a decision soon.

The problem is that the BTL buyer is at Stage 4, while the ATL buyer, Mary, with whom you might have had a fleeting conversation, is at Stage 2, and you now have this nasty thing called separation (see Figure 11–2).

Your options now are to:

1. Hope Bob has the skills to sell Mary, the ATL buyer, and convince her to get to Stage 4.

2.   Arrange for you and Bob to go to Mary and review with her what you and Bob have been doing, but since this is all BTL stuff, her interest will be low at best.

3.   Go over Bob's head, get a meeting with Mary, and ask her what she wants in a solution from you, but she doesn't really care, which is why she has Bob on her team.

So these options are really not good options at all, but they are what you have allowed for. This is a common scenario, unfortunately. Instead of racing through Stage 2, when you were so excited to meet the need criteria of Bob, you should have honored The Split.

IT'S NOT A RACE

When we look at stages and the amount of time spent in each stage, we typically see something like this:

Typical Sales Timeline

Stage 1	Stage 2	Stage 3	Stage 4	Stage 5	
3	3	5	7	2	Days total: 20

Let's assume this is a $15K sale. Twenty days plus or minus is a good total for a deal of this size. If it were a $5K deal it should take fewer days, and if it were a $100K deal, it would probably take more.

And when we look at the days spent in each stage, this model looks pretty good, plus or minus a few days here and there.

However, this model is flawed in a few areas.

1.   You blew through Stage 2 and did not honor The Split.

2.   Because of that, your Stage 3 was really only a demonstration to the BTL buyer. The ATL exec may have been there, but all you discussed was BTL stuff.

3.   Stage 4, if you had done your job correctly, would not have taken as long as it has, since by Stage 4 you and the prospect have agreed on what you are doing, and a proposal at this stage is only validating what you have agreed upon.

4. When a deal like this one matches this timeline, you can pretty well guess that at Stage 4, the salesperson has presented the proposal to the prospect, and the prospect has said to the salesperson, "Thanks, this looks good. We'll get back to you."

5. Control has now passed to the buyer, and the salesperson is waiting, bugging the prospect (remember Dan D's "harass" stage?), and trying to figure out what size discount to offer the buyer to entice her to sign.

A better twenty-day sales process should look more like this.

Better Sales Timeline

Stage 1	Stage 2	Stage 3	Stage 4	Stage 5	
3	7	5	3	2	Days total: 20

When you honor The Split, you need the time to understand both value propositions and quantify them both. The need to spend more time at Stage 2 is obvious.

What are the proper sales goals of Stage 2? We have talked about The Split, and the need to go to both ATL and BTL to find the two value propositions. An important part of that effort is finding out about the famous Three Qs (well, not famous now, but by the end of the chapter . . .):

▶ The Quantified Problem (QP)

▶ The Quantified Cause (QC)

▶ The Quantified Solution (QS)

THE QUANTIFIED PROBLEM

Below the line, most prospects are looking to solve a problem they have been handed. This problem is what has driven the BTL buyer to come up with decision criteria. It's what they want your solution to do, so they can get what they want, get their problem solved (Solution Box A), and contribute to solving their boss's problem (Solution Box B).

This decision checklist can be organized, again by the Five Ps: Product Features, Perceived Quality of Fit, Professional Support/Ease of Use, Price to Value Ratio, and Personal Win, which you remember from Chapter 3.

Product Features

The features and benefits discussed with a product or service usually help the person who is going to be using or in charge of the success of the purchase, so it's typically a BTL requirement. They want answers to questions like:

▶ How's it going to work?

▶ How big is it?

▶ Can it interface to X, Y, and Z?

▶ How long till it's up to speed?

▶ How do I service it?

▶ How much are supplies, and where can I get them?

BTL buyers need these answers before they can make a recommendation to the executive level. BTL buyers are the ones who are responsible for this purchase, and the product features are going to determine the success or failure of the product with them.

Perceived Quality of Fit

Quality is very important to the person who is going to be using a product or service on a daily basis; it's a key part of what a BTL buyer buys for. How well is it made? How well will it perform? How does it compare to other similar products, and is the quality difference worth the price difference that is being asked? Does it do everything I need it to do, or am I making compromises?

The perceived quality of a product or service breaks down into five areas:

Basic Need Quality: The basic ability of a product or service to answer a need is important to the BTL buyer.

▶ Can it meet the need?

▶ Is the quality good enough?

These considerations may be overridden by the ATL exec, based on their perception of the importance of what is being purchased and how it affects their Trains.

The BTL buyer usually wants the best her budget can buy, and sometimes will make a demand for even better quality of fit, and will either try to get more budget money or obtain a discount from the vendor.

> *"Our requirements are pretty unique. Not all the vendors can do all of what we want. We have to meet a lot of needs, and it's got to stand up to the most rigorous tests."*

Top Quality: If the ATL buyer consents, the BTL buyer can go for the best. The perception of top quality can be influenced by a number of factors, including brand awareness, prior usage, familiarity, and referrals. However top quality is understood and documented, and whether it is real or perceived, some BTL people have a perception of "the best" and want to make sure they get it.

> *"We need the best, no questions asked. This is a critical decision, and we just can't afford for anything to go wrong."*

Commodity Quality: Sometimes, a product is deemed somewhat of a commodity, and therefore as long as it meets a standard, then all things being equal, any choice will suffice. Products and services of this type include televisions, printers, lawn mowers, belts, food items, airplane travel—anything that is seen as interchangeable. Does it really matter if you fly United or American? If it was the same price and you got the same miles credit, and both flew at the same time, would you really care?

> *"We see everyone the same, even though some might be a bit better than others. The difference in quality is really negligible."*

A buyer who says this sees all vendors as more or less equal and will probably buy for other factors than quality.

Time Quality: Time quality issues have to do with short-term vs. long-term time frames. The buyer will ask himself:

- ▶ How long will we keep it?

- ▶ How long will we use it?

- ▶ How long does it have to last?

- ▶ How long will it be until something comes up that replaces it?

- ▶ How long do we have to put up with it until something else better comes along?

These are questions a prospect asks when they view quality over time. The astute salesperson addresses these quality/time issues.

"You'll only need this for a short time until we can figure out a permanent solution."

Regulation Quality: This quality is an assumed quality, since it is either formally or informally regulated. Think soap, prescription medicine, UL electric standards of quality, FDA quality standards for fish and meat, FAA standards for flights. This type of quality goes to the extremes. Either a company says they meet the minimum at a lower price than most, or they far exceed the minimum but at a reasonable price. It is rare to find mid-level quality for mid-level prices.

Professional Support/Ease of Use

This category concerns the ease of doing business with the vendor, the service and support the selling organization will provide. It can take many forms, including hand-holding, training, the certification process, customer support, installation, warranty servicing, ease of returns, repairs, 24/7 support, the educational experience upon purchase, help with the user interface, and instruction manuals and documentation.

BTL buyers want to feel they will not be all alone when something breaks. They want to master the new product or service with a learning curve that should be short initially but will grow with their usage.

The need for professional support/ease of use for the BTL buyer sounds like this:

"This better not take me a long time to learn how to use. Also, if I need assistance while I'm using it, will there be someone to help me?"

If you want a discount at a retail clothing store, you cannot expect the same kind of service, ease of checkout, and tidiness of dressing rooms as you would get at a high-end retail store. The manual and instructions for the $3,000 computer TV will be very different from those for the $129 tablet. BTL buyers expect service proportionate to what they believe they are paying for quality. The salesperson would say:

"You are asking for help desk and chat support. Both those services are available for you."

"You want a company who can provide platinum service. We can offer you the best in the industry."

These are three examples of how you can make professional support/ease of use an advantage for you. What are the things you offer that can fall into this category and be a competitive weapon?

Price to Value Ratio

Quality always has a price. It also has a budgeted amount for the BTL buyer. Buyers always want the maximum for what they can afford, but "maximum" is different for each buyer, based on their weighted decision factors. BTL buyers will pay more for what they deem important to them rather than pay for overall quality.

One buyer may feel that the quality of the documentation is well worth the price. Another may want a certain color, a certain interface, or even a particular style or brand that they believe more than justifies the price.

Budget is something the ATL gives to the BTL person, so based on the BTL's ability to get more money, she will see her budget and features as a balance of what she pays for and gets.

Personal Win

The well-documented "What's in it for me" syndrome is generally foremost in the mind of the BTL buyer.

Whether it's a promotion, a raise, more responsibility, a chance to look good, something to make the job easier, a chance to make the job better, or the opportunity to join an exciting or high-visibility project—

most BTL buyers have a WIIFM mentality, even if they really believe they are acting in the best efforts of the company.

In ranking order, WIIFM ranks as:

1. WIIFM in terms of getting rid of a problem.

2. WIIFM so I can get some praise and recognition today.

3. WIIFM in the future.

BTL buyers usually live in today, so getting rid of a current part of a job they hate or giving them something that makes them good right now usually does the trick.

THE QUANTIFIED CAUSE

We discussed the importance of finding out what is causing the ATL exec to change from what they have been comfortable with. Something specific is happening to cause them to expend resources and spend time and money on something.

You need to know what. When you find that out, you need to quantify it. ATL execs always use numbers. Always.

"This is a big investment for us."

"We are really excited about this."

"I feel if we can get this done, we will make a huge impact."

Without numbers, these emotional words will lose energy near the end of the buy/sales process. You need to get numbers. I just can't stress this enough. ATL execs are really comfortable with numbers, since they deal with them every day.

"This investment will require 60 to 70 percent of our resources."

"This commitment will affect at least 20 percent of this year's revenue potential."

"I feel if we can get this done, we will increase profits by $300K this year alone."

BTL buyers usually do not have the full story. Their vision—and their responsibility— is more limited than the ATL buyer's, so they really can't give you true numbers. The ATL exec always deals in numbers, and the sooner you quantify the cause, the better you can craft an ROI to Solution Box B and the part that you can play in it.

THE QUANTIFIED SOLUTION

The proposal you will be putting together—with all the options and the final price or price options—is your solution. It has numbers in it, so it is your quantified solution.

The point is that if you are going to give a quantified solution, which you always do, you should Give/Get a quantified problem (BTL) and a quantified cause (ATL), so all the numbers add up, and you can quantify the investment value to both value propositions.

It's time to gather all that we have learned so far, and sum it up in a story. Let's call it the printer story.

PRINTER STORY: THE VALUE OF THE THREE Qs

In our office, we have an office manager named Ann. She has been with us for many years, and she does all the things needed to keep the office functioning. She assembles the workbooks for our training classes (some of which are around seventy pages long), she does the billing, all the A/R, monitors the checking account, pays the bills, and basically keeps the office functioning. She's an important part of the team.

A few years ago, Ann came into my office one day and proclaimed, "We need a new printer!" Not knowing what to say, I asked, "What's wrong with the old one?"

She went on to describe her problems. "It doesn't print as fast as it used to, it jams and breaks down quite a bit, and the supplies are getting hard to find."

So I ask, "Okay, how much for a new one?"

"About $1,000," said Ann.

"What, $1,000?" This was a few years back when the economy wasn't really strong, and spending money made me nervous.

"That seems like a lot of money. Times aren't really great right now. Can you make do with what you have for a few months more?"

"I guess I can," she replied.

Whew, dodged that bullet. Imagine spending $1,000 on a printer. Well, I just bought a delay of six months, and by that time, I hope the printer will have fixed itself or something. At least I don't have to deal with it now.

A few weeks go by, and one Monday, I get into the office late, about 11:00 A.M. I walk in, and Ann is at her desk, on the phone, and she's in tears.

"What's wrong?" I ask.

"The printer broke again. I've been on the phone with HP for at least twenty minutes, and I can't get it to work. You have to be in San Diego tomorrow and need twenty-five books and I can't get them printed. FedEx comes at 4:00, and if they're not ready by then, you won't have them for tomorrow.

"I am so frustrated right now, I don't feel I can do my job the way I want to. I'm not sleeping at night because I'm so stressed about not being able to do my job. My husband retired a year ago, and I should have retired with him. I don't need this job and all the stress . . ." and her words faded into a blur.

So now, I have two problems. Problem #1: I may not have books for my program tomorrow. Problem #2: Ann is not happy. I really don't want her to quit. So I make a decision. "Ann, what are you working on? Spin it off to a USB drive, and let's go down to Kinko's and make the books there."

We get there, use their printers and copiers, put the books together, box them up, put a label on them, and by 3:45, we are done. Project complete. Problem solved.

We leave Kinko's, and I turn to Ann and say, "Ann, you are so right. We need a new printer. You now have a budget of $1,000. Go get yourself a new printer."

A couple of days later, after returning from San Diego, I go into the office and see Ann at her desk with a big grin on her face.

"What's up?"

"I've found a new printer for the office, and if it's okay with you, the salesperson would like to have a word with you."

No problem, I'll try to get a better price! A few minutes later, Ann calls out that the printer salesperson, Jimmy, is on the phone. I pick it up.

"Good morning Mr. Miller, I'm Jimmy, and I'm working with Ann to get you the printer you need. I think Ann and I have found one that meets your needs, so let me tell you a little bit about the printer.

"This is our new G2000 printer. It's our latest model. A few key things you should know about it are:

1.   It's our latest design. It only needs three color cartridges. Older styles have four or five, and ours only has three. It's highly efficient.

2.   Additionally, its throughput is thirty-two pages per minute. The one you have currently is a twenty-pages-per-minute printer, so this one is over 60 percent faster.

3.   Additionally, Ann being the smart shopper that she is, has opted for the 500-page drawer option. The printer comes standard with a 200-page drawer, but Ann feels she needs the 500-page drawer, since you can put a whole ream of paper in and not have half reams floating around the office."

I don't know what a ream is, and I certainly didn't know I had a ream problem in my company, which I guess we do, so this 500-page drawer will solve that ream problem—good. I tried not to feel lost.

"The price on this printer, all done, is $1,200."

You can imagine how much I knew about or really cared about three cartridges, thirty-two pages per minute, or a 500-page drawer. Nothing. Didn't know what they meant. All I knew was we were $200 over budget.

"Jimmy, that's great, but all we have is $1,000 budgeted. What can we do on the price?"

"Oh, Mr. Miller, that's our best price," on and on.

Time out. Do you think I cared about three cartridges, thirty-two pages per minute, and a 500-page drawer? That's right, I didn't. However, Ann does care, since she is the BTL buyer. Here are some reasons why she cares:

1.   If you don't know, color cartridges are not cheap. We don't stock them. So when Ann needs one, she has to get in her car, drive five minutes to the closest Office Depot, and hope they have one. Well,

if she has to do this less often with this new printer, that's a WIIFM for sure.

2. Ann is paid a salary, not an hourly wage. So if Ann has a pretty big job, she has to wait for the printer to print all the books before she can go home. Sometimes she's at the office until 6:00 or 7:00 waiting for the printer to print, and doesn't get anything more than my thanks. But if she gets this new printer, she doesn't have to wait for the pages to print, and she can be home on time.

3. And, man, solving that ream problem is huge! I really didn't know paper has weights and color brightness levels, and that Ann would never mix reams of paper, because according to her, mixing reams would make the workbooks look less than professional.

Okay, there you have it, the quantified problem (QP):

▶ 3 cartridges

▶ 32 pages per minute

▶ 500-page drawer

These mean very little or nothing to me, but mean a lot to Ann, the User Buyer, the BTL buyer. To her, the QP means a lot.

When Jimmy had me on the phone, what should Jimmy have asked me? He should have asked about *cause*.

He should have said, "Hi, Mr. Miller. I've been working with Ann and I think we found a new printer that's just perfect for you." Okay, it's multiple-choice time. Which of the following question should he have then asked?

A. What is causing you to look at the G2000 printer?

B. What is causing you to look at printers?

Of course, the correct answer is B, since I'm an ATL buyer, and not interested in a G2000, G3000, or any letter anything thousand. If he had asked, "Mr. Miller, what is causing you to make a decision on a printer?" I probably would have told him, "Jimmy, Ann is an important part of our company." What I would not have said was, "And I can't afford to have her quit in despair."

Ann had retired (temporarily) a few years earlier. We hired a replacement who, within a few months, ended up not working out.

We had paid a recruiter $2,500 to find Ann's replacement. We also had paid Ann $2,500 to stay for a month or so and train the replacement. Flash forward to the present: If Ann does quit over this printer issue, I'm looking at a potential additional $5,000 expense. Additionally, if Ann does walk out the front door over this printer, who has to assemble these books? That would be me, and I'm really busy during the week, so I'm now looking at weekends.

$$\text{Quantified cause} = \$2,500 + \$2,500 + \text{weekends}$$
$$\text{Difference to budget: } \$1,200 - 1,000 = \$200$$

So now, based on Solution Box B, ATL value, it looks like $5,000 and some weekends vs. $200 extra. Watch how fast I order that printer. The formula you want to solve in Stage 2 is:

$$\text{Quantified Problem (QP)}$$
$$\underline{+ \ \text{Quantified Cause (QC)}}$$
$$= \text{Quantified Solution (QS)}$$

Jimmy never asked me about the cause, so we negotiated to $1,100 and got free shipping as well. He never found out the other value proposition—the ATL value proposition. He was so focused on Solution Box A, the BTL Solution Box, that he left a lot on the table.

QP—3 cartridges, 32 pages per minute, 500-page drawer

QC—$2,500 + $2,500 + weekends

QS—$1,100 and free shipping

Solution Box A: $1,000 budget

Solution Box B: $5,000 and a few weekends

Figure 11–3 illustrates The Split in this story.

Figure 11–3 Bringing It All Together: The Printer Story

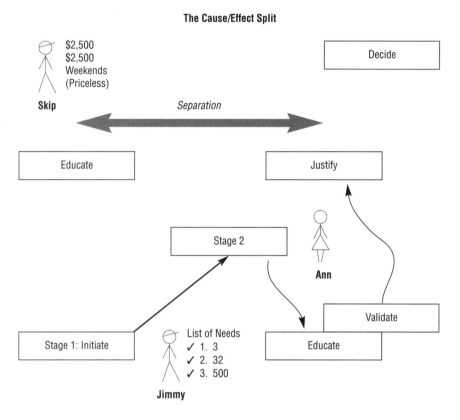

I would have bought the printer at list price, plus a year's worth of cartridges, and an additional twelve-month warranty if I'd had to.

Give Jimmy credit, though. He did get to the ATL exec, and the deal was done in a fifteen-minute phone conversation, which goes to the speed issue and energy issue when you're dealing with ATL. Ann was worried she was not going to get a printer that was 20 percent above approved budget, and she really wanted that printer.

Cause is a great tool to start your dialogue with an ATL executive. There is more you can do when you are at that level to take the conversation even deeper, to really find out what specific issues the ATL exec is having, and how to address the value equation. You do that with the ValueStar, discussed in the next chapter.

CHAPTER 12

Discussions with an ATL Executive

The vocabulary that an ATL executive uses is very different from that of a BTL user. Why? Because BTL buyers focus on technical and user-specific requirements, while ATL buyers focus on business and fiscal requirements.

Salespeople are generally trained really well by their companies to speak to the BTL. They get:

▶ Product training

▶ Competitive training

▶ Company history and competitive advantage training

▶ How to use the product training

▶ How to get things done in the company training

But where is the ATL training?

THE VALUESTAR: LEARNING ATL VOCABULARY

This section is a primer to help you gain vocabulary skills so you can speak to the ATL buyer, based on a tool I've developed called the ValueStar (see Figure 12–1).

It is imperative that salespeople learn ATL vocabulary, since speaking any other language to an ATL exec is ineffective and a waste of your time. For the ATL exec, there are five ways of creating value:

▶ Return on investment (ROI)

▶ Time

▶ Risk

▶ Leverage

▶ Brand/Image

Figure 12–1 The ValueStar

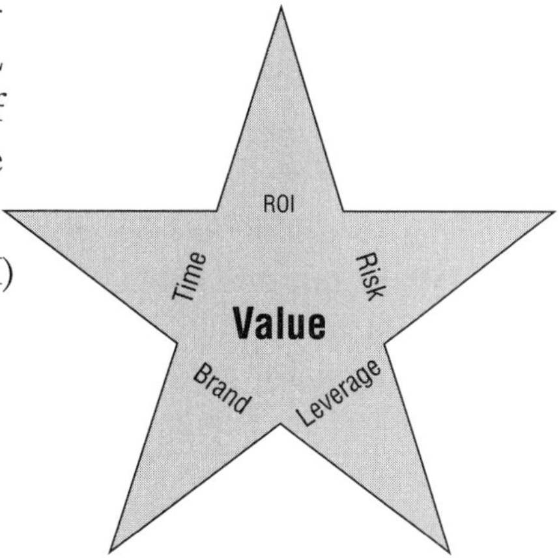

That's all. These five areas are the keys for you to increase your ATL vocabulary. Study these five points, write them down, and under each point, create questions you could ask an ATL exec. The ValueStar is about asking the right questions, not speaking to execs about what your product or service can do.

The ValueStar is a unique way for a salesperson to arm himself ProActively and sell what the buyer is asking for, not what the seller wants to sell them.

ROI: SELLING MONEY

Return on investment (ROI) is near and dear to most companies' hearts. It's the common term companies use to quantify what is important to them. Companies are always trying to increase revenue and decrease cost to reach their annual and quarterly goals. Making a profit and investing those profits to grow the company is the reason a company exists. Businesses want to grow profitably, and to do this, they must get a return on all their investments and invest only in projects that will return an approved ROI.

What do you sell? Really, what do you sell? When we ask salespeople this question, we usually get answers like:

- ▶ Services
- ▶ Solutions
- ▶ Advantages
- ▶ An easier way of life
- ▶ Value
- ▶ Features and benefits
- ▶ A better way of doing something
- ▶ Competitive advantages

Okay, you ready? The list above is for the BTL buyer. At the ATL level, you sell money. That's it. One more time: You sell money.

ROI dominates most ATL discussions, and most of those discussions are about numbers. When an exec is involved in a purchasing decision, it's what does it cost, how does that help my Solution Box B (Trains), and what is the ROI going to be? Execs usually have an official guideline they need to get on investments. They want to get back two to three times the money they are giving you so they can invest that money into other ideas so they can make even more money. It sounds simple, and it is, and it is based on the premise that you sell money.

LEARNING ROI-SPEAK

One of our clients sells an annual service, paid monthly. They look at revenue monthly, so monthly reoccurring revenue (MRR) is the key metric. For this subscription-based service, they charge their customers anywhere between $2,000 and $20,000 + per month. They talked to some of their executives and tried to figure out why they did not have very successful exec-to-exec meetings. The client's VP of Sales explained to me:

"We looked at our slide decks, and all the features and benefits we were discussing, all the tools we take on sales calls, and we realized that it was all about us—all of it.

"So we talked about preparing more of an ROI discussion. What could we do when at the ATL level to have better outcomes? Could we whiteboard it and make it interactive? We looked at formal and informal ROIs our customers said they were receiving by using our stuff, and then incorporated that into a set of discussion points.

"We realized to senior people in the prospect's organization, we were just an investment they were making. It seemed that they looked at our services differently than the users of our services were looking at us.

"Our users loved working with us and what we did, and how we supported them, and that was the value proposition we were most proud of. That story never resonated at the ATL level, though. Hey, we are very proud of our world-class customer service, our methodology, and our quality. Our users love and appreciate a lot of things we do and improve upon. ATL buyers, though, they want different outcomes, since they look at things differently. They view us as an investment, and they are interested in only one thing; how they are going to get their money back. What is the ROI on the investment they are making? Oh, I'm sure they like us and think that what we do and what we provide is really helpful, but all they care about is their investment.

"As a matter of fact, now that we know we need to take a financial look at what we discuss with ATL execs, we have seen a tremendous rapport on most calls we go on. We ask them what they want as a return on this type of investment—their goals and the kinds of financial outcomes they are looking for this investment to bring to the table."

When we talk with that company a few weeks later, the VP of Sales described the changes they had made, and the success they had:

"We have had about a dozen ATL discussions, and we think we are getting better after each one. We're talking about the product less and less, and more about the ROI. As a matter of fact, many of the senior salespeople have heard us a few times, and they are starting to ask ATL questions, which is great."

It's funny that most companies don't teach their sales teams to speak this language. They are so caught up in the features and benefits of what they are selling that they rarely ask about how their client intends to pay for it.

"Pay for it? They cut a check or give me a credit card."

"The purchasing department can issue a PO. We then send an invoice, and the customer then writes us a check. That's how it works"

The more time you spend with an ATL executive, the more chance you'll have to get a decision quicker and increase the average sales price (ASP) or average order price (AOP).

There are two important rules about ROI.

Rule #1: There is a difference between a subjective ROI and a quantified ROI. You have to quantify the Solution Box or Trains the ATL person says will be affected by what they are buying from you.

> *"This will increase the investment we are making in the channel by 3 to 5 percent."*

> *"I can see how this will be worth two to three months to the project— this year!"*

> *"The return on this investment is worth it. I can see how this will contribute to the doubling of sales."*

Rule #2: ATL numbers come from ATL buyers. Sure, they will look at all the spreadsheets and literature you want them to look at, but that will be to validate what they are thinking. Most ATL execs can tell you a few things about what you are offering:

1. What Trains your proposed solution will affect. How much those Solution Boxes are worth to them.

2. Approximately what you are worth on each one.

3. If your investment is worth it, marginally worth it, or not worth it at all.

If they can't tell these things, there is no current Train that they are working on for which your solution can be a fit—or you are talking to the wrong person.

MAKING THE MOST OF TIME

Time is the second point in the ValueStar, and one of the most used points on the star. Time has many dimensions to it, and a salesperson needs to look past their single point of reference for time.

There are many ways companies try to measure or quantify time. Anyone will pay for time, including you. You will pay more to drive on a toll road in order to avoid taking a jammed freeway during rush hour.

You will pay more to take a nonstop flight if travel time means a lot to you. I know that when I travel to Europe, I always try to take a nonstop. It's usually a bit more, but then I don't waste a day trying to get over jet lag, so it maximizes my time when I'm there.

Your prospects will pay to be faster as well. Companies always pay for time. Companies face many different time challenges. If it were straightforward, it would be easy. One ATL exec's time issues probably are tied into another's time issues, so you should probably ask time-based questions about organizational issues or projects that are currently being looked at.

Companies have many time challenges, deadlines, time to market, and financial market issues. Your job is to find out as much as you can about the time issue your prospect faces, especially as it relates to their Trains.

Customers have only twenty-four hours in the day, seven days in a week, fifty-two weeks in a year, like you do. You cannot cheat time. There is no getting around it. Since it is a scarce and valuable resource, prospects value it highly. Find out what is important to them. Improving timing can mean:

1. Getting a new product to market before a calendar deadline.

2. Getting a new product to market before a compelling event (trade show, overseas customer conference, financial briefing, etc.).

3. Getting new pricing out before the end of the quarter.

4. Meeting the scheduling for an upcoming reorganization.

5. Responding quickly to a social media campaign that has had an immediate impact, positive or negative.

6. Meeting goals managers have set with their bosses that involve a time element.

7. Doing anything in less time to minimize use of the planned resource.

8. Getting new packaging out to make the year successful.

9. Getting a new product to market before a competitor announces a me-too product.

10. Successfully addressing customer successes or complaints.

You want to have multiple questions about timing when you go into a meeting. Make sure you can address multiple time-value issues.

There is a second part to time, and that's Time-Travel. All ValueStar questions need to be asked in a Time-Traveling, three-dimensional way.

It's not going to do you any good to ask ValueStar questions in a two-dimensional, "today" format.

So time on the ValueStar has two uses: addressing ATL time issues and Time-Traveling. It's important, no, it's *critical* to get time right.

RISK: THE MILLION-DOLLAR QUESTION

If you want a topic that will get some immediate attention, it's risk. Wikipedia says:

> Risk is the potential of losing something of value, weighed against the potential to gain something of value. Values (such as physical health, social status, emotional well-being, or financial wealth) can be gained or lost when taking risk resulting from a given action, activity, and/or inaction, foreseen or unforeseen. Risk can also be defined as the intentional interaction with uncertainty. Risk perception is the subjective judgment people make about the severity of a risk and may vary person to person. Any human endeavor carries some risk, but some are riskier than others.

Now take a look what they say about business risk:

> The term "business risk" refers to the possibility of inadequate profits or even losses due to uncertainties—e.g., changes in tastes, preferences of consumers, strikes, increased competition, change in government policy, obsolesce, etc.
>
> Every business organization contains various risk elements while doing business. Business risk implies uncertainty in profits or danger of loss and the events that could pose a risk due to some unforeseen events in the future, which causes business to fail.
>
> For example, an owner of a business may face different risks, as in production risks due to irregular supply of raw materials, machinery breakdown, labor unrest, etc. In marketing, risks may arise due to different market-price fluctuations, changing trends and fashions, errors in sales forecasting, etc. In addition, there may be loss of assets of the firm due to fire, flood, earthquakes, riots, or war and political unrest,

which may cause unwanted interruptions in the business operations. Thus business risks may take place in different forms depending upon the nature and size of the business.

Business risks can be classified by the influence by two major risks: internal risks (risks arising from events taking place within the organization) and external risks (risks arising from events taking place outside the organization).

Look at all these risks! BTL buyers rarely are exposed to these challenges, but this is what ATL buyers are expected to weigh when they make a decision. When you open Pandora's Box and ask risk questions, you had better be prepared to:

1. *Listen* to their response.

2. *Clarify* their answers and questions. If you are selling something that would affect the marketing department, ask, "What risks do you see in marketing's plan for the year?" rather than "What risks do you foresee for the year?"

3. *Guide* the conversation to uncover current Trains the ATL executive is working on—that is, their top priorities.

4. *Summarize* what you have heard the ATL exec say.

5. *Gain agreement on the next step.* Ask, "If there was something that could mitigate some of these risks, would that be important to you?" Then propose a next step both parties should take to validate that you can deliver what you say you can, and then quantify the return your product/service will offer.

When risk questions are asked correctly, you'll hear comments like:

"Right now, I've got a fifty-fifty confidence on the go-to-market project we are working on. If you can do what you say you can do, I can see that getting closer between 80 and 90 percent."

"The new system needs to be up and running by the tenth of next month, and the risk of that date slipping is between 60 and 70 percent"

"Launching our products with an additional distribution channel is risky. I see risk of losing 10 percent of our current sales if this launch doesn't go perfectly."

If you are looking for a point on the ValueStar that rises above them all, then you need to master the risk questions. You must talk, understand, and assist the prospect in addressing and mitigating their risks—by executive persona, by industry, by geography.

Value can mean different things to different people, and the objective and subjective nature of ROI and time can be debated. Will they save that much time? How do they know they will actually get that kind of ROI? What if the schedule slips? Subjectivity and qualitative factors start creeping in, and the question becomes for the ATL exec, "How do I know where to put the stake in the ground?"

Risk is the key value factor that keeps ATL executives up at night. Decisions at the lower levels of the organization are pretty black and white—yes/no, now/later, up/down, switch/don't switch, in/out.

Decisions at the more senior levels of companies are never that simple. These decisions have too many tentacles that reach out into the organization, which is why these decisions need an ATL exec to be involved in the first place. Senior management decisions are much more complex and take into account so many other factors—that's why they are fraught with risk! Risk abatement is what makes the senior executive turn her head and take notice.

"With the resources we have, is this the smartest decision? What are the risks we haven't thought of?"

"Okay, what have we forgotten? Is there a competitor out there that we have overlooked and therefore makes our go-to-market decision riskier?"

"Is there a potential risk between our profits and our customers? If this product does not do what we say it can do, it will mean six to eight months of lost revenue. Have we covered all the risks and weighed them carefully?"

ATL execs always talk about risks; it's what they do every day. They need to discuss it since it's their neck they are sticking out. Salespeople come in and they ask questions, but are they ATL risk questions? They ask:

"How do you see our relationship between our two companies going forward?" (Reactive and hoping for direction.)

"Can I give you an executive company overview so you know who we are and what we can do for you?" (All about you.)

"Are you the decision maker on this project? If so, can we have twenty minutes of your time next week?"(So I can beg you for the order and not really listen to your issues.)

"We have been working with the IT department, and as the user, we just want to make sure you see what we are selling." (Maybe you can convince the IT group to hurry up.)

"Do you have the final authority on my deal?" (My favorite . . . NOT!)

Although these are questions we are always asking, they do not address the ATL's risk on the Trains they are working on, so you will not get much ATL attention. Risk is the lead area you should be asking questions from.

The confidence factor attached to risks is where you want to aim your questions, which is why these decisions and the risks ATL execs face will motivate them to grant you the time you want.

"What do you see as the biggest risk in your goals over the course of the year?"

"What are the risks relative to product launches that you face in the next three to six months?"

"Have you thought about the risk of doing nothing on this current initiative?"

"What would a successful implementation look like, relative to the risk you are taking?"

"What do you see as the major challenges and risks you have with this project?"

ATL executives want to talk to you about risk. They need to find answers and mitigate some of their risks, since the more risk they take on, the less confident they are about the outcomes. Salespeople come into the office and try to sell something, usually speaking about features and benefits, spewing out a feature/function (remember the three cartridges, thirty-two pages per minute, and a 500-page drawer?).

For the ATL exec, it's about value. They really care about the risks their Trains may face, and how they can launch and maintain those Trains with the least possible amount of risk.

ATL mangers confer, meet, discuss, talk about, think out, and make decisions about risks. That's what is expected of senior management. For every decision and investment they make, for every act they justify, they have to weigh the risks. Discuss with an ATL buyer making their Trains more sure, or less risky, and you will have their attention.

LEVERAGE: BUILDING VALUE ACROSS TRAINS

Leverage is the part of the ValueStar that reminds you that ATL executives build value across projects, not just on one project. Multiple Trains are in the station (see Figure 12–2). Your conversations should have at least some impact on more than just one.

The conductor of Train 1 may have brought you in, and you may get some time with the station master (the ATL exec). But once you are in, you should certainly sell to the conductor on Train 1, but don't stop there. Also ask for other Trains the ATL station master may have had problems with over the past six months, or Trains that may have trouble making their scheduled departure in the future. (AWAY questions plus Time-Travel in one go. Congratulate yourself for pulling this off!) You

Figure 12–2 At the Station

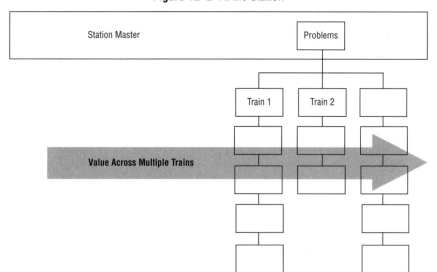

want to ask questions about ATL initiatives and find a way to leverage your company solutions across multiple (two or, better, three) Trains.

> Gary sells for a company that manufactures surfboards. He called on Jack, the VP of Operations at a big retail company.
>
> Gary had two options:
>
> 1. Tell Jack how much he values the business on Train 1, which he had established with the conductor of Train 1, Mike, and then go over the company's other products that might be a good fit.
>
> 2. Thank Jack for the opportunity and find out what Trains Jack has in his station house over the next six months.
>
> Gary took option #2, and found three other Trains that Jack had on his desk he needed to get moving, and Gary's company could help a lot with one, a little with two, and a pretty good amount on the third. Gary's company is now a value-added supplier to Jack, not just Mike. He is also selling more to Jack, and Jack is getting more value.

It is really scary for salespeople to go to a meeting armed with nothing but questions. They feel naked. If they don't have their slide show, printed materials, customer success stories, samples, or at least a leave-behind, they feel awkward and ask:

"Why would this senior manager take time to meet with me when all I do is ask questions and hunt for Trains? I better have a backup plan!"

Well, yes, backup plans are never a bad idea. But your backup plan should not be BTL stuff. Stay above the line and hunt for Trains. Exercise the leverage that comes with your access to power by asking about multiple Trains.

ATL execs need answers to their challenges, issues, problems, tasks, and concerns. They have to solve these challenges, since new ones will be arriving daily, and they would rather talk about their challenges, issues, and problems than your products and services.

BRAND/IMAGE: THE EMOTIONAL VALUE

From our friends at Wikipedia again:

> Brand is the "name, term, design, symbol, or any other feature that identifies one seller's product as distinct from those of other sellers." Brands are used in business, marketing, and advertising.
>
> . . . A brand defined as an intangible asset is often the most valuable asset on a corporation's balance sheet. Brand owners manage their brands carefully to create shareholder value, and brand valuation is an important management technique that ascribes a money value to a brand and allows marketing investment to be managed.

Brands/Image has value, and many ATL decisions base their value return on this point of the ValueStar alone. A brand is what makes a company's product distinct from all the rest. Image is a reflection of the likeness of something. Brand/Image includes quality, since quality is usually in the eye of the beholder, and is more perception than reality. Brand/Image takes shape in the form of:

▶ The product you sell

▶ The service you offer

▶ The benefits

▶ Being seen as successful

▶ Being seen as a decision maker

▶ Being seen as a front runner

▶ How your customers perceive your company (*outside view*)

▶ How your employees perceive the company (*inside view*)

The list of elements that make up a company's Brand/Image is endless. Value is very individualistic. Emotions and perceptions play a major role, and you need to discover what is really important to each buyer in the prospect's organization.

Emotional ownership—on a personal or organizational level—transfers with Brand/Image.

Discuss with your prospective customer what your product/service will do for *their* Brand/Image. If you can improve their competitiveness, make them look better by associating with you, or lessen risk for *their* customers who buy their products, you create leverage and create value. Does the IT organization have a terrible brand inside the company that you can help them with, in addition to the features and benefits of what you are trying to sell them? Think from your customers' perspective as well as yours.

A Final Word About Asking ATL Questions

You may find yourself in a meeting where two languages are being spoken—that is, you may have both ATL and BTL people in a meeting at the same time.

When a BTL buyer is in a meeting with an ATL exec, you need to speak above the line. If the manager is any good, she knows she must understand her boss's requirements. How many times have you been in a meeting with both sides and the BTL buyer only wants to talk feeds and speeds, and the ATL exec starts fidgeting and mentally checks out of the meeting?

How about the meeting where there are three or four BTL buyers, and they gang up on the ATL exec, trying to force a decision, only to have the ATL exec ask a few ATL questions, which the BTL buyer can't understand? There's the end of that meeting.

Smart BTL buyers know the ATL exec comes at the solution in a different way. They attack the solution from the perspective of value. Think of the ValueStar as the ATL questioning guide. It's where ATL questions come from.

When you have an ATL exec in the room, ask great value-based questions. By asking ATL execs Time-Traveling ValueStar questions (yes, mentioning Time-Travel one more time), finding their Trains, and showing you can move the chains for them, you are going to shorten your sales cycle and increase your selling price, guaranteed.

CHAPTER 13

Creating and Controlling ATL Energy

We have discussed the two different value propositions we have called Solution Boxes. Solution Box A is for the BTL buyer, and Solution Box B is for the ATL buyer. Trains are just another name for multiple Solution Box Bs, since the Station Master is ATL. It is also important to know not only what value there are in Trains, but where the "Train Stations" are, so you can find these Trains.

In Silicon Valley, where I live, you hear about a lot of new companies eager to find revenue—so eager, they must make sure their value proposition is well understood. We get quite a few calls that go like this:

"Skip, could you help us define our value proposition? If our potential customers could just see our value prop, then they would understand why we are so valuable."

We then agree to a meeting, where they bring out their slide deck.

▶ *Slide 1*—Company name and fancy logo.

▶ *Slide 2*—Who the founders are.

▶ *Slide 3*—Their value proposition. Why they are so uniquely qualified to be in the market.

▶ *Slide 4*—Always the map slide, showing the globe and where their offices are. (FYI: this is a *particularly* stupid slide.)

After three or four slides, I stop the person showing the slides, and draw these stick figures (Californians with sunglasses) on a piece of paper.

The seller is trying to sell the buyer something, and the seller is convinced that if the buyer can just understand the seller's value proposition, then they will see the light and make a purchase decision. But it doesn't work that way, and here's why.

The buyer has a customer, either internal or external. An example of an internal customer might be an IT manager who services the sales organization, creating a sales forecast for the CFO. An external customer comes into play for a CFO who serves analysts in the financial community.

The buyer's role—BTL or ATL, it doesn't matter—has now changed—from buyer to seller—since he has a customer. The real value to the original buyer is not Value Proposition A; it's Value Proposition B.

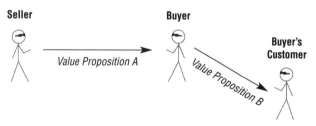

If the resale need of the buyer can be met with Value Proposition B, then Value Proposition A has even greater worth to the buyer. Only if the buyer's *customer's* need can be met will Value Proposition A actually be of any value.

An example of this "dual proposition" would be selling a lead generation service to a Chief Marketing Officer who has to increase revenue

(Value Prop A) while keeping the leads at 10,000/month, and staying within the 5 percent marketing budget the CFO has set down (Value Prop B).

Most salespeople, however, seem to think that all value lies in Value Proposition A, which would be feature/benefit selling (2-D) and it's really not their fault. The company only really teaches Value Proposition A, thinking that's their unique value proposition. It's what makes them unique and why they beat out the competition (back to BTL feature/benefits again). If sales, when selling ATL, would focus on Value Proposition B, asking questions about Value Prop B, getting numbers for Value Prop B, imagine how much more they would sell.

THE GOLDEN RULE

The golden rule of selling above the line has two parts:

1. AWAY leads to energy.
2. Questions lead to transfer of ownership.

The AWAY approach focuses on finding out what is causing the change—what is causing the ATL executive to change the way he or she has always done things. There is energy in this change.

Questions can be causal questions, ValueStar questions, or even basic Time-Traveling questions. Let's explore both energy and transfer of ownership a bit more.

Each sale has three energy sources: the salesperson, the ATL buyer, and the BTL buyer. When a salesperson uses all three, she can increase the sense of urgency about the sale, increase the value and the average sales price, and be on track to get a decision faster than in normal deals. In this chapter, we're going to look at the energy that you bring to the sale.

THE SALESPERSON'S ENERGY

The general rule of thumb is that energy for a deal must come from the customer. After all, he is the one with the money and the need. He is the one dictating the pace. So if a deal is to get more energy, it must come from the buyer. Makes sense? Not necessarily.

There are numerous ways a salesperson can create energy for a sale. Here are some of the more obvious ones.

The Law of 2X

There are only two ways to shorten a sales process.

1. Cut the sales call from thirty minutes to twenty minutes. While this will result in shorter meetings, it probably won't put a dent in the overall sales cycle length.

2. Shorten the time between sales calls. You do this with the Law of 2X.

The Law of 2X says that most salespeople give their buyer *twice* as long as they really need between steps in the sales process. If you address this problem, you can shorten the process, effectively creating energy.

Listen to Karen ending a sales call.

"Jerry, that's great. I think we have had a great meeting, would you agree? So as a next step, why don't we get together and look at some options. This is Thursday. How's next Tuesday or Wednesday sound?"

Karen did a good job proposing a next step, but why did she say next week? Not many good things can happen by waiting this long for a next meeting.

▶ Energy will start bleeding. Most people have "fires" that come out of nowhere and start to consume their day.

▶ Jerry's boss may have a fire, and Jerry will have to delay some of his current projects.

▶ A competitor may come into the sale and either take control or make them an offer they "can't refuse."

There are a lot of things that *can* happen, and most are not good for the sale. One of the biggest reasons Karen pushed the next step out three or four days is her fear of rejection. She doesn't want to hear the customer say no, so she puts the day way out into the future, when the prospect probably has some free time.

"Jerry, let's get together tomorrow."

"Karen, I'm swamped. The earliest I have is next Wednesday or Thursday."

"Oh, sorry, no problem. Is Wednesday afternoon good?"

As soon as Jerry pushed back and said basically "no" to Karen, a couple of things happened:

1. Karen has been rejected, feels that Jerry is superior now, and that she has given control over to Jerry.

2. Karen is reactive now; she'll do what the customer tells her to do.

This is bad. The customer may be in a position to say he is busy and can't see her, but if this deal is really important, maybe Karen can convince the prospect to "move a few things around."

"Jerry, that's great. I think we have had a great meeting, would you agree? So as a next step, why don't we get together and look at some options. What's early tomorrow look like for you?"

"Karen, I'm swamped. How's next week?"

"Jerry, I think you would agree this is important. I don't see this taking more than ten or fifteen minutes. Could you carve out some time, say around 8:00 or 8:30? I'll bring the coffee."

It doesn't matter if Jerry can or can't. What matters is Karen has applied the Law of 2X, and she will be able to:

▶ Shorten the time to a decision if Jerry agrees because she asked for it. (But you really *do* have to ask for it.)

▶ Requalify the client. If this is truly important to him, he'll move some things around if he can.

▶ There will be no energy bleeding or competitive window. The faster she can get this to a decision, the better, as long as she is doing all the right things during the sales process.

The Law of 2X says that most salespeople want to give the prospect more time since they don't want to come off as pushy. Asking for a meeting "sometime next week" really has the opposite effect. You don't want Jerry thinking,

"Karen must be busy this week. Too bad. I had time on Friday, but I guess next Wednesday or Thursday will work."

What do you think would have happened if Karen had proposed that same afternoon (Thursday), or the next day, Friday, at the latest? You got that right; she might already be celebrating the sale!

Take control of the sale in between steps, shorten them up by half, and you will be creating energy for your deals.

Sales Process Control

Buyers want to be led. Most of the buyers salespeople meet do not have a degree in buying stuff. They are a VP of Engineering, VP of Manufacturing, CMO, COO, CFO, and the like. Even the VP of Sales is usually a lousy buyer. These people went to school to do what they do best. Buying something is probably part of what they do, but it's not the main thing, unless you are constantly selling just to purchasing agents.

As a ProActive salesperson, you have a map. You know that buyers follow the sales process step by step. You know where you want to go, all the time. You can call it "next-step selling," ProActive selling, or just being one step ahead of the game. Just remember: Buyers want to be led.

In some cases, there are formal buy processes laid out. Okay, sure, but that doesn't mean you can't take control by adding things at every step, like homework assignments or Time-Traveling discussions.

Additionally, you may have to add some steps based on what the prospect has to do, for example, when there are legal requirements. You can think of many reasons why you are not in control, and how buyers want to "take the lead" in a sale. It's been our observation, though, that even in organizations that believe they have to react to the buyer, the good salespeople in that company don't play by those rules. They know how to take control and lead a buyer through a process.

Control the process, and you can control the energy.

Define the Sales Process with Journey Maps

Another way to control the process and create energy is to develop a Journey Map, which is like a AAA Trip-Tik, with the prospect.

The American Automobile Association (AAA) offers a trip-planning tool called a TripTik. Long, narrow ring-bound pages lay out your journey. If you are in Chicago and want to go to Miami, you call AAA and they send you a series of maps—probably close to thirty for that trip—showing how to get from point A to point B as you journey between the two cities, with details about restaurants, hotels, parks, and special attractions along the way.

It's smart to use this same philosophy with buyers, who want to be led. Since between 65 and 70 percent of people are predominately visual learners, consider creating a Journey Map of the sales process, a visual sequence of events similar to the one shown in Figure 13-1, and keeping it handy.

How to Develop a Journey Map
Develop a Journey Map in a three-step process.

Figure 13–1 Journey Map: Work the Buy/Sell Process Together

January		February		March
Launch Details	Finalize Requirements	Key Meetings	Purchasing Requirements	Vendor Selection

Initiate Engagement · Key Mgt. Presentation · Final Negotiations

What Does the Customer Have to Do?

1. _____
2. _____
3. _____
4. _____
5. _____
6. _____
7. _____

What Do We Have to Do?

1. _____
2. _____
3. _____
4. _____
5. _____
6. _____
7. _____

☐ Critical Dates for ABC Company ☐ Critical Dates for Us

1.   Compile a list of things the prospect has to do between now and when they are going to make a decision.

2.   Then develop a list of things each of you—you and the buyer—have to do between now and decision time. The prospect's list should always be longer than your list.

3.   Once you have the completed lists, map them out on either a horizontal or a vertical axis.

Basic Journey Map Rules

1.   Make sure you work *with* the prospect to develop this. This must be a joint effort. If you do all the work, there is no transfer of ownership.

2.   However, the prospect will be happy for you to be the one with the master file and the one to do all the updating.

3.   Only send files to the client that they cannot update. It's all about your keeping control.

4.   You can create an ATL Journey Map or a BTL Journey Map (one for each buyer), or one that combines the two levels.

5.   Journey Maps should end with an implementation date (I-Date). Do not end it with a "contract signing" date (that's selling language, not buyer's language). Near the end, the Journey Map can be extended to the first thirty or ninety days after the I-Date to complete the transfer of ownership.

Most salespeople understand what this tool is, but most don't take the time to use it. It's an unbelievably effective transfer of ownership tool, and a great way to control the sale. You may want to try it sooner rather than later. Figure 13–2 shows what a specific Journey Map might look like.

You and the client are going to follow a process. The choices are the client's process, your competitor's process, or yours.

A visual sequence of events that the BTL prospect can constantly show the ATL executive is going to make the BTL buyer (and you) look very good. It's a journey that you control.

Figure 13–2 Journey Map for Blue Sky Industries

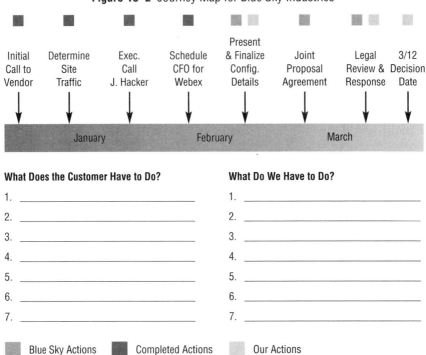

Initial Call to Vendor	Determine Site Traffic	Exec. Call J. Hacker	Schedule CFO for Webex	Present & Finalize Config. Details	Joint Proposal Agreement	Legal Review & Response	3/12 Decision Date

January   February   March

What Does the Customer Have to Do?

1. _____
2. _____
3. _____
4. _____
5. _____
6. _____
7. _____

What Do We Have to Do?

1. _____
2. _____
3. _____
4. _____
5. _____
6. _____
7. _____

■ Blue Sky Actions ■ Completed Actions ■ Our Actions

Trumpeting in Stage 2

In Chapter 8 we discussed trumpeting, the sending out of emails or social media messages to senior executives before you start working with the BTL prospect. Here are suggestions for two additional trumpets.

Trumpet Update

A trumpet update alerts executives of the company that some work has been done; you are giving them updated information. To do this effectively, you must keep it short, factual, and, again, nothing about you yet. This is a straight business transaction, and if they want to know what you do, they can look you up on the Web.

So what does a trumpet like this do? It keeps them in the loop, it's factual (Marketing has asked IT to fix something), and you are building up ATL rapport. It is really important that you stay neutral here. No pitching, no selling. Give them status of what's happening, since ATL execs love status updates.

Dear XXXX,

After discussing with John Gates in IT, we came to some basic conclusions:

- There is a reason for us to continue conversations about solving a current problem that affects marketing and IT.

- Our next step is to determine if the marketing requirement that has been requisitioned from IT can be satisfied with some of our tools.

    This is a first step, and we wanted to keep you in the loop. We'll let you know more about this later. Thanks in advance.

Skip Miller

Account Manager, XYZ Company

It's great if you get a request from one of them to send you some more information. If you get a request to stop sending you these emails, you have three choices. You can:

1. Stop trumpeting.

2. Send an email back explaining that typically companies are really excited to see the ROI we provide, and executives get blindsided by requests for funds that have not been budgeted. All you are doing is keeping them informed.

3. Send an email back saying you will stop. Add that this process is proceeding, and if you can be of any further help, here's your contact info.

However, if you want to keep trumpeting, that's up to you. It is a really good way to create energy inside a prospect's organization.

If the BTL person says to stop sending these ATL messages, ask them why. All you are doing is providing a progress report and making them look good in the process. Ask the BTL how they would want to change it—have them coauthor or be copied or acknowledged? Stopping probably is not a good thing, and it may disqualify the entire account.

Trumpet RFI

Another form of creating energy with trumpeting is the request for information (RFI).

Dear XXXX,

After talking with John Gates in IT and looking at your website, it seems there may be an opportunity for our company to help address some issues you're having.

Is it possible to have a fifteen-minute conversation where you outline your initiatives for the next three to six months so we can make sure the work we are doing with your organization has its desired effect?

I'll call you in a few days, or you can let me know what time works for you, say Monday through Wednesday of next week?

Regards,

Skip Miller

Account Manager, XYZ Company

Okay, so it's a little forward, but you are now addressing ATL executives, and asking for their time. Not for the standard dog-and-pony show, but for a reason, a very good reason. Your product can help solve an ATL problem, contribute to one of their Trains. That's why they are looking at you in the first place. Problems within companies usually spread to multiple departments in organizations, they all talk about them at senior staff meetings, so make sure you just don't send out a Trumpet RFI to just one ATL exec.

You can gamble that the BTL buyer fully understands exactly what the ATL buyer's problem is and what they are looking for, or, you can go straight to the horse's mouth and take fifteen minutes and ask the ATL execs yourself. You can create ATL energy this way, or you can rely on the BTL person, who probably does not know the ATL value proposition and how it can affect other Trains.

You can guess which way I think you should go (yup, the horse's mouth it is). We'll look at some specific tools and techniques to help you harness ATL energy—and BTL energy as well—in the next chapter.

CHAPTER *14*

The "How" of Controlling the ATL Sale

The theory of why you need to split the ATL and the BTL sale is now becoming obvious. The "how" of getting this done is another thing. By using some of the tools and ideas in this chapter, you will feel better prepared and more confident in your approach.

ATL ENERGY: FINDING ADDITIONAL TRAINS

Another way to create energy in a deal is to hunt for multiple Trains. There are numerous ways to do this; one of the best is to trumpet email to all other execs, telling them what you are working on and its expected benefit, and asking if they would like to be involved. This is really effective when:

- Your boss writes the letter (it's coming from a higher authority).
- You reference examples of how a company purchased what you offer, and in no time, others wanted in on the experience.
- You co-write the letter with someone in the prospective company.

This can slow a sale up by getting more people involved (negative energy), but it can also speed the process up since it's now getting more executive attention. This tool is a gamble, but one worth taking under certain circumstances. Unfortunately, I can't tell you what those circumstances are; the answer is it always depends, so you'll have to develop your own instincts.

Energy from the ATL buyer can come from many sources. The question has always been, "What's causing this ATL buyer to change what they have been doing and look for a different answer? What broke?"

The fastest way to create energy with an ATL exec is to discuss their current initiatives and the challenges they are having with them. ATL energy is currently being expended on these Trains, and the faster you can discuss with the ATL exec what you can do to help, and the faster engage with you in this dialogue, the faster additional energy will become available.

The Focusing Power of Deadlines

Deadlines stimulate energy. The closer the deadline is, the more people involved in the deadline, the more commitments being made because of the deadline, the more energy the deadline will have. There are many types of deadlines, including:

▶ Product deadlines

▶ Fiscal deadlines

▶ End-of-month/quarter/year deadlines

▶ Contract deadlines

▶ Sales deadlines

▶ Employment deadlines

▶ Market opportunity deadlines

▶ Contest deadlines

▶ Response deadlines

▶ Commitment of resources deadlines

All organizations and all ATL execs have deadlines for their Trains. In most situations, the ATL exec is meeting these deadlines; otherwise he wouldn't be any good at his job. However, generally a few Trains are not doing great, and with deadlines approaching, those are real issues for the exec—and can create wonderful potential for your product/service.

> "Deadlines refine the mind. They remove variables like exotic
> materials and processes that take too long. The closer the deadline,
> the more likely you'll start thinking waaay outside the box."
> —ADAM SAVAGE

Roll deadlines into the Time-Traveling ValueStar questions you should be asking anyway. Just make sure that when you ask these questions, you listen for time-sensitive Trains and for deadlines. Time questions are about value, and the deadline questions are like a turbo-boost of energy. There are two different energy sources here, so uncover and use both.

Revenue: Building Value Across Trains

Revenue is one of the true metrics of a business. ATL execs sometimes put market growth (revenue) above profits if they are on a mission to grow market share at the expense of short-term profits.

Revenue, net revenue, sales, net sales, gross revenue—all these terms refer to the same thing: money. There is a reason that revenue is the top line of the income statement. It's usually the first question someone asks.

"So how big is your company?"

"What's your annual revenue?"

"What are your sales figures for this year?"

Money is related to perceived power. It's about being the gorilla in the market, and that perception is usually based on revenue, revenue growth, and expected revenues. The bigger the company is, the bigger the opportunities for salespeople.

Show ATL execs that you will help them obtain revenue, and you will find energy. Many salespeople want to try to show the ATL exec how what they are offering can save costs. While that's important, ATL execs have a ton of options at their disposal to cut costs. That stack of papers on their desk is quite large.

Options that help them increase revenue, however, are valuable since that stack of options is generally really short, and since revenue growth and top-line performance are important, the topic of revenues will get their attention.

Find Trains that they are working on that are revenue producers, and ones they are having some challenges with. Identify these opportunities and you will gather energy.

Gaps: Business Energy Providers

In business as in other parts of our lives, there is often a difference between goal expectations and achieving those goals; this difference is what we call a *gap*. It's these gaps that keep the ATL exec's Train in the station, where it can get help. If a Train faced no gap, then it wouldn't be in the station; it would be out making money.

Gaps are what ATL execs measure to find out how they are doing relative to achieving their goals. It's a term that is common to all ATL executives, but it is rarely used by salespeople.

ATL execs talk in gaps daily. Why? Because all their goals and initiatives have a quantified number associated to them. They say things like:

"We need to get $20M more in revenue."

"We have an opportunity to beat projections by 25 percent."

"This has to cut costs by 15 percent by the end of the year."

"We have to get five more market share points."

"Our response rate needs to be 80+."

"Our A/R average needs to be less than sixty days."

"The customer satisfaction score has to be above 90 percent by the end of April."

All lines of business—sales, marketing, finance, IT, manufacturing, engineering, HR—have numbers or a timeframe, or both, tied to them. That's how they know if they are accomplishing and contributing to the company's bottom line.

It's a funny thing about the goals that ATL execs focus on: They're rarely on track. They're usually a bit behind (and occasionally a bit ahead) of plan. This makes sense, since if a goal were on plan, it wouldn't get much attention from the ATL exec.

All initiatives are being measured. Use the gaps in these measured goals to create value.

Time Adjustments Are an Opportunity

Initiatives and goals are usually measured monthly, quarterly, or annually. ATL execs need to take a "temperature check" on their initiatives to see how far above or below their plan target they are. If they are above the plan target, are they maximizing the opportunity? If they are below plan, can the gap be made up? Add deadlines into the mix, and look at the energy available in these gaps.

You need to use these pauses, these reviews, to have a conversation with your prospect to demonstrate to them that you can speak to them on a topic that is near and dear to their hearts—their goals and the difficulties in meeting them.

Gap Charts

A Gap Chart is a tool for getting the ATL meeting focused on the company's goals and initiatives, and for quantifying their problem and your value.

All ATL execs have goals and initiatives, and there is often a gap between current performance and a goal. That gap is usually above or below the stated objective. Let's say you have a prospect that has a $20M goal for the year for a new product launch. If you ask, six months into the goal, how they are doing, you will hear one of three responses:

1. *"Great, everything is positive. There actually is some potential upside."*

2. *"All right. We are on track."*

3. *"It's going to be tight, but we are probably looking at a deficit of $500K."*

The ATL exec who gives the second response—we are on track—will not want to talk about this issue, since it is doing fine and needs little attention. No energy there. That Train has left the station and is running fine.

Figure 14–1 Gap Chart

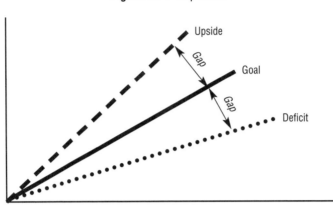

What you are looking for is the ATL executive who answers with the first or third response. Why? Because they are looking for answers! If they had the answers, they wouldn't be talking to you. They need help closing that gap (see Figure 14–1). They need some energy.

ATL executives live in a quantified world that's all about numbers, so to have them quantify the gap means value for you and your solution. What this means to you is if you are going to have effective conversations with ATL execs, you have to talk numbers . . . and it's *their* numbers they care about.

"We have the runway for a 10 to 15 percent upside."

"If we do this right, we should be able to go past the number by a couple of million."

"To do this right and hit the goal, I see us right now coming up between 15 and 20 percent short."

Once you have a gap that needs to be addressed, you have some choices. You can fill the gap for the prospect—that would be a push. Or you can have the prospect fill the gap for you.

"So Mr. Hardeman, what are the one, two, or three things you are working on to close the gap?"

At this point, the prospect will describe the things they are working on. However, they still do not believe these things will fully close the gap, since if they did, they wouldn't be talking to you.

"I need to get my salespeople selling larger deals, ramp my new hires quicker, by at least two months, and open up the London office at least three months earlier than planned."

Now you ask the prospect what he thinks will happen if those possibilities materialized, were completed, were accomplished.

They usually say that an increased amount or the whole gap will be made up. This is the time for you to say you can assist with helping to close the gap. When you show an ability to move the chains on this initiative, you have a great chance to get the order quickly.

ATL execs want to talk about their gaps. They want to solve their problems or obtain their goals, and if you can help them even a little bit, they are going to give you and your proposal special consideration, since all your other competitors are pitching products and hoping something sticks. Make it about revenue, and you get extra energy.

Think about it. In a meeting with an ATL exec you have two choices.

1.   Tell him who you are, what you are doing with his BTL managers, and hope he sees value in what you are doing.

2.   Ask him/her what their problems are over the next three to six months, listen for gaps, show how you can contribute to help close these gaps, and create value. (This effort rarely involves any discussion of the first point.)

Imagine Nick, a Chief Marketing Officer, sitting in his office. It's the end of the quarter. There are some issues he is working on, and he needs to address his goals, objectives, and commitments—and earn his paycheck.

He is reviewing his annual objectives right before your meeting. He notices a few Trains that are looking good, and a few that need work. Hmmm, he'll have to come up with some ideas.

In your meeting with Nick, you have the following conversation:

"What are you looking at in the next six months, and what do you feel most at risk for? "

"It's the new product rollout. I've committed a $10M revenue figure for the first nine months, and it looks like it's going to be short."

"How short do you think?"

About 20 percent."

You have your gap (see Figure 14–2.)

Next, you ask him what he is doing to close the gap. Usually, executives will come up with two or three solutions they are working on.

"Well, I'm working on getting more channels involved, adding a separate product to pull sales through, and offering the sales team added commission to really get their attention."

Think of gap-closing initiatives in terms of inventory. There are three types of inventory: raw materials, work in progress (WIP), and finished goods. The place you want to have a discussion is WIP. Why?

Raw materials is a can of worms since it needs approval from other lines of business and the executive committee. Ideas in this area would take a Herculean effort to get on board.

Finished goods is an area where the initiatives are working fine. Why bring them back into the Train Station for reevaluation?

That leaves WIP. The WIP initiatives the ATL executive is working on need some added support or these initiatives would be in finished goods, right?

So, any initiative that's in the WIP category needs some help (or it would already be in finished goods)—and if your solution can help, you will find yourself dealing with one happy and eager ATL executive.

Figure 14–2 Nick's Gap Chart

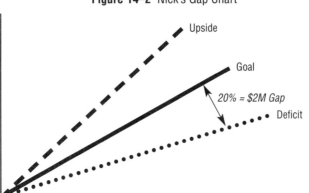

You need to qualify and quantify the exec's initiatives. You continue the conversation:

"So Nick, right now, you still feel you would be 20 percent short of the goal with your current effort. However, if you could make substantial progress on getting more channels involved, adding a separate product to pull sales through, and offering the sales team added commission within the next ninety days, how would you feel about the 20 percent gap?

"If I could make some progress with more than I am currently doing in the next ninety days, I think it would make up at least half of the 20 percent."

"That's what I think we can help you do."

Move the chains. You are not the answer, but can help get them closer to realizing their current goals. You can help them get their current ideas, still baking (WIP), launched into finished goods, or at least a little closer. All they have to do is listen to you for a bit longer to see if indeed you can really help. They'll give you the time.

You have now done a few things:

1. You've identified the crucial initiatives that the prospect is working on, for which of course they do not have final answers to or they wouldn't be working on them.
2. You've gotten the prospect to assign value to his initiatives.
3. You've said that you can *help* with the initiatives and get them closer to completion. You are not the answer, just part of the answer.
4. You've put yourself at a competitive advantage. Your competitor has not tied her solution to this initiative, and that will cost her big time. You are now addressing the value proposition above the line.

If the cost for your solution is say, $100K, the ATL exec is going to weigh the $100K investment to the overall $2M. At this point, do you really think he cares if your solution costs $100K or $120K?

Also, you can always bring initiatives into the conversation in question form if the prospect is not covering an area that you offer. They may have not thought of an initiative that you know might be of some help.

"Those are good items, Nick. Have you also considered new packaging schemes or appealing to a different buyer?"

Since these are areas you can help with, you probably want to bring them up so you can judge if they even would consider them as options (disqualification). It's like priming the pump.

A Gap Chart is a great tool to be used with an ATL exec. It rarely works with a BTL buyer, since they are only doing what they have been told to do, and do not have control over the options like an ATL buyer does. The Gap Chart quantifies value and attacks the area of most concern to the executive-level buyer, the items that will "keep them awake at night" over the next three to six months, and that they have to get off their desk. It's a place of energy.

Being Reactive and ProActive on Gaps

Use Gap Charts as early as possible with a prospect. It will show the ATL exec you have come to the table with ideas and a problem-solving mentality. You can wait until the ATL brings up what they are working on, or you can be ProActive and plan to work this tool as soon as you can in the sales process.

If you are still gun-shy about using this tool, try it out on some of your current customers. They know you and will be forthcoming about what they are working on, and who knows, you might even pick up some more business while perfecting a new tool.

BTL ENERGY

ATL energy is very important to a deal. The motivation for most deals comes from ATL, and therefore, most of the prospect's energy will come from ATL. However, there are some BTL energy sources that should be looked at to make sure we don't leave any potential unexplored.

Since the BTL buyer is doing what they have been assigned to do by the ATL (the one with the problems and the money), you can use the BTL's enthusiasm, her popularity within the organization, and her reputation with the ATL to get energy.

In many sales, the BTL does have the authority and the budget to make a decision. The Five Ps (see Chapter 3) will help you get to energy sources that are important to the BTL buyer. In many cases, a weighted ranking of the Five Ps can uncover where the BTL buyer's energy really is.

Let's say there were one or two Product Features that the BTL buyer just "has to have." These would be a source of energy, and you should show how you can deliver in these areas.

The BTL buyer may already be familiar with the Professional Support you offer, and may find it sufficient. But you can still create energy here, perhaps by showing what you can do with advanced users. Letting them talk to your engineers about new product ideas or inviting them to be beta test sites may create energy as well.

If you tell them you might even want to film them talking about their success or do a webinar with them on a panel discussion, you will surely create energy in the Personal Win area.

"Why Wait?" Questions

Time is always an energy source. The BTL buyer is on a timeline. You are tapping an energy source when you ask why they are waiting. It's important that you treat their waiting as if it were a concrete objection instead of dismissing it with, "It's just how they make their decisions."

Way too many deals are just stuck in time. The BTL buyer feels helpless to make a decision; it's out of his hands, or she's too overwhelmed with current obligations to launch something new—the "I'm too busy to try to get ahead" syndrome.

"Why wait?" questions will break down excuses and bring more energy into the deal.

"Why are we waiting for Ed? Is he your boss?

"What would happen if we didn't wait?"

"How can I help Ed catch up?"

"What can we do in advance so we are all not waiting?"

"What small step can we take right now to show progress and not have this thing stall?"

There are other devices you can use to create energy and shorten the time to a decision. Let's take a look at Journey Maps, I-Dates, and more.

Journey Map Reviews

When you have a Journey Map, you can accelerate time and gain speed and energy.

The Journey Map is a tool that will help the prospect stay on course, help you control the sale, and keep the competition out. During the sale, you should constantly keep the Journey Map updated. The larger the sale, the more you might add items that have nothing to do with your sale, but that mean a lot to the overall project from the customer's point of view.

For example, you sell office furniture, and a prospect's 5,000-square-foot expansion project means a $40,000 sale to you. Your Journey Map could have not only your furniture and systems included in it, but might also include associated products and equipment that you don't sell, like the laptops for every desk, the movers who will deliver the front office tables, and even the move-in date for the first employees. The more you make it about their project, and less about your product/service, the more control you have and the more important you will be to your prospect.

Expand the energy you get from a Journey Map by calling on the power of I-Dates, the idea that Buyers Buy Backward (BBB), and special offers (not really recommended).

I-Dates

The implementation date (I-Date) is a very important concept. It is when the buyer implements or installs what they have bought. The purchase date is something the seller remembers, but buyers really only care about the I-Date.

▶ Do you remember the date when you bought your spouse's gift, or the date of his or her birthday?

▶ Do you remember when you bought the vacation, or when you went on it?

In business, buyers know their go-live date—the moment when whatever they bought from you is up and running.

You can move I-Dates based on production schedules, availability of resources, and the like. Here are some examples of how you can move I-Dates.

> *"Harry, I've got some good news. Our key installer has just had a job postponed. If you guys are ready to make a decision two weeks earlier than planned, we might be able to get our top installer for your project."*

> *"Jennie, we have a truck in your area next week that has some capacity. We might be able to get you some material by Tuesday of next week. Do you have any jobs you want to get done early?"*

> *"Keith, I know you have said you want this up and running by March 1. What would happen if you could get it up by February 15 and save two weeks?"*

By moving I-Dates, not your sales or contract sign date, you can create energy in an account from the BTL level.

BBB

Remember That Buyers Buy Backward.

> *"My anniversary is November 5, so that means I need a gift by the first, which means I need to go the mall the weekend before, which means I need to ask her sister what she wants this week."*

> *"We need to have the new product shipped by the 17th, which means we need the new machine in and in production by the 11th, which means we need to make a decision on this new machine by the end of the month."*

Buyers always work backward from a date, and you can use this energy to shorten or lengthen the time it takes to close the sale. Go backward from their I-Dates and see what you can help tighten up, or what you can add value to or eliminate. Perhaps you can even sell them additional services earlier than planned for, as long as it's mutually beneficial.

With both I-Dates and BBB, the BTL buyer has a large say; he or she can influence the ATL buyer if there is something that is of value to them and will save them time. For example, getting things done faster so there is potentially less risk would certainly appeal to an ATL buyer.

BUYER WORDS

The BTL looks at everything as an expense; after all, the potential deal is an expense item on a budget that's been given to them. These are the words you know and love.

The ATL words look at everything as an investment (you're selling money, remember), so get used to these words if you're going to have ATL conversations.

BTL Words		ATL Words	
Cost	Price	ROI	Value
Expense	Budget	Risk	Time
Afford	Pay	Invest	Return

Since you're going to be hanging out with ATL execs as well as your old BTL buddies, you should know the right vocabulary to use with each buyer.

Special Offers

You can also generate energy with special offers—discounts, end-of-the-month deals, special packaging, and certain promotions.

Remember Gives/Gets from Chapter 7? There, we presented it in the context of ATL homework, but its reach is great. It has become standard practice for the salesperson to assume the buyer must want something ("Give" a discount) in order for the salesperson to obtain something ("Get" the deal). In truth, discounting and special promotions are becoming too standard. Does anybody do a list price deal anymore?

If you look at value from the ATL and BTL buyer's perspective, they are certainly getting a lot already. When you are working with two value propositions—not just one, as most salespeople do—the need to offer special deals at the end of the sales process will diminish greatly. You should be looking at how to create energy for both the ATL and the BTL buyer, since that really does create a win-win for all parties, and that's what good salespeople strive for.

A good way to transition to the upcoming chapter on mutual value is to make sure you understand what value means to the ATL exec and the BTL buyer—and by now you realize they are very different creatures, each with their own vocabulary.

CHAPTER 15

Stage 3: Value vs. Value

Your company employs you, and hopefully you like it there. If you re-member the first few months of your employment, it was really exciting. It was like you had a USB cable plugged into your head, and the infor-mation you were getting on who you were, your value proposition, and how you could beat the competition was great. You were wondering why your prospects couldn't see all this information as clearly as you could.

We know it doesn't work this way, and the reason is that you and the prospect are in different stages. You are in the Validate stage, and your prospects are in the Educate stage (review Chapter 2 if "Validate" and "Educate" merely ring a distant bell). For them to feel like you do, you need to get them to Validate.

FORGET ABOUT THE USB 4.0 CABLE

You joined the company you are with for a lot of good reasons. You've been there for a while, and you are really good at knowing why you and your company are one of the best in the business.

"If I could just have my prospects see what I see and know what I know, their choice of a vendor would be obvious."

(continues on next page)

It's like a USB 4.0 cable (which doesn't exist—well, at least not yet). If you could just stick the cable into your prospect's head and download what you know into their head, of course they would buy from you.

Being proud and confident that you have a great solution is not really why people want to buy from you. The "Let me tell you how it is, let me tell you how this works" doesn't work with employees, kids, or spouses, so why do you think it will work with your sales prospects? It's because it's what we've been trained to do.

Think about it. Before you joined your company, you were in the Educate stage and were looking at all the opportunities and were questioning whether you should pull the trigger and leave your former job. Once you made your decision, you then wanted to feel good about it, and once you had those first few weeks under your belt, you went from Educate to Validate. You now are listening to things about your company to validate your decision to change jobs. You are specifically hearing things and seeing things that reinforce your decision.

TWO VALUE CONDITIONS

When your prospect goes to Stage 3—Validate, they need to go from the first "I get it" to a second "I get it." That is, both the ATL and the BTL buyer need to have their two value conditions met.

The first Value Condition, the first "I get it," is satisfied when the buyer understands what you are selling. They are educated. They get what it does. They understand or have figured it out.

The second Value Condition is realized when they *really* "get it"; that is, they see how it can be applied to what they need or what they are doing.

The brain cannot educate and validate at the same time. When the brain is educating, it is trying to figure out how it works, what it does, or what it all comes with. Validation occurs when the buyer relates the good or service to what they want to do with it, and the satisfaction they will derive with the purchase and use of what is being sold.

A classic example is buying shoes. You see a pair of shoes you like. They are the right color, price, and style and come from a manufacturer you have bought from before and trust. You have just *educated* yourself on the shoes, and have asked to try a pair on.

You validate the shoes when you try them on, look in the mirror, and think about when you will be wearing them (our good friend Time-Travel). Will they fit the occasion? What will other people say if they see them?

You can think of other simple examples as well:

▶ Buying a car

▶ Buying a TV

▶ Buying a house

And I did recently buy a house, and it wasn't until I found one with a backyard I liked and could imagine throwing the family parties in that I was ready to go to contract. Time-Traveling had validated that this was the house for us.

The First "I Get It" Condition

The BTL buyer is really focused on your features and benefits. He is trying to determine what's really important and whether what he chooses can satisfy the needs checklist. He doesn't want to come up short, so he wants to make sure the car has power steering, automatic transmission, Bluetooth-ready stereo, and heated seats (Quantified Problem).

Getting the BTL needs checklist is easy. It's usually been developed and approved by either their ATL boss or a committee. The BTL buyer usually has some idea of what he wants, since he will be the one using it. It's rare that BTL buyers have no idea what they want. They typically have been doing the job a certain way, and what you offer is a better way, but the results of the job, the outcomes, will still be their responsibility. They have some experience at what they will be required to do, and some idea of how they want to do it better.

For the ATL buyer, the first "I get it" comes when she understands that what you are selling can make a dent in one or more of her projects

(Trains). She sees that you can fill a void or help close a gap. I need to get transportation for my daughter so she can go to school, or I will still have to take her every morning (Quantified Cause).

The Second "I Get It" Condition

The second "I get it" at the BTL level is when the buyer gets to try it out. He takes "ownership of the solution." Some examples:

▶ Taking the car for a test drive. This simulates their day-to-day driving habits and they are validating it will fit the bill.

▶ Seeing a demo with his own data loaded.

▶ Having a whiteboard discussion on how it will be installed and launched in the first thirty days.

▶ Going on a user visit and seeing it in operation.

The list is endless. This is all part of the regular sales approach and is usually reserved for well-qualified deals, since it is considerable work for the sales team to prepare and execute.

The second ATL "I get it" comes when she sees the product/service will move the chains on one or more of her Trains. Not only will her daughter get to school using the car service, but the exec will be able to spend two hours more in the office, not have to work overtime, and be able to start those EMEA meetings earlier, which is what she wanted to do months ago.

What most salespeople miss is the two "I get its" at the ATL level. The salesperson has an executive meeting and usually does one of the following:

▶ Gives them an executive overview of the selling company and what it is all about.

▶ Gives them an update on what the salesperson is doing with the BTL buyer inside their company.

▶ Asks them what keeps them awake at night (two-dimensional, a big no-no).

These are not terrific options, but since most salespeople have never been ATL executives, they usually focus on what they know and have experience with, rather than what's important to the ATL executive.

THE SALES REVIEW—THE WRONG WAY

Sales Manager: "So, John, tell me about the deal."

John: "It's for twenty of our doodads, so it's worth about $20,000. I talked to the senior VP, and he said they really need this to be competitive in the market, so we have a value match at the executive level."

THE SALES REVIEW—THE RIGHT WAY

Sales Manager: "So John, tell me about the deal."

John: "I talked to the ATL executive, and he told me about his top three goals for the year. He has some major gaps in two of them, and can quantify about $500K in revenue he will not see if he doesn't do something different. We talked about some options, and scheduled a next meeting to go over some of them. There was a point where he asked me, 'So you're tell me that if we go ahead with this purchase, I'll see a major impact in my lead generation initiative as well?' When he said that, I knew he really got it."

The wrong way was all about jamming a solution to the ATL executive almost regardless of what the problem was. The right way was a problem-solving approach, and then validating that the salesperson could possibly offer a solution to at least one Train that was mutually agreed to by the ATL executive and the salesperson as having value, and having the ATL realize it in their own words.

To express it as a formula, it's:

$$\text{Goals} + \text{Gaps} + \text{Options} = \text{Quantified Cause}$$

You really have to dive deep into:

▶   What is important to them.

▶   Why it is important to them.

▶   How you can be part of the outcome.

A DAY IN THE LIFE . . .

A look at a day in the life of an ATL executive is in order. Looking at how an ATL executive thinks and works will give you some insight on how you should sell to them, and how to help him "get" both Value Conditions.

ATL Time Frames

An ATL executive operates at three levels—long term, midterm, and short term. The *long term* is their strategic vision—what they need to do over the course of the next twelve-plus months to make sure they contribute to the overall vision of the company.

Some examples:

▶ A CMO agreeing to a 20 percent increase in Net Promoter scores over the next twelve months.

▶ A VP of Engineering agreeing to shrinking project development time on new products by 5 percent over the next three projects.

▶ A CEO committing to a 5 percent market share growth over the next eighteen months.

These long-term goals are important, since most ATL's bosses will hold them accountable to these goals.

In the *midterm*, the ATL exec chooses among the things, tasks, and projects the ATL executive has committed to for the accomplishment of the long-term goals, the Trains. Usually, these midterm options are incomplete and need some attention.

Some examples:

▶ A CMO launches a new social media campaign to boost leads from 1,000 per month to 1,500 per month. Doing this allows CMO to show progress on the long-term goal of increasing revenue from new customers by 30 percent year over year.

▶ A VP of Engineering agrees to train 20 percent of the engineers in the organization in a new process of design, since that will contribute to the goal of shortening lead time by 10 percent over the next six months.

▶ A CIO invests in a new analytics/big data process since the overall reporting goal for the year is a 50 percent decrease in reporting time.

Short-term activities are in the nature of events. They are things that come up that are probably not scheduled but need attention. Budget money isn't really funded for these, but if a need is important enough, money will be found. The opportunity window on these events for a salesperson is pretty tight, since a short-term goal needs to be addressed immediately.

▶ A VP of Sales, recognizing that revenue will be off for at least the next two months, makes a rapid investment in a new lead-generation process that can ramp up inside of ten days.

▶ A CIO gets a new acquisition streamlined into the IT infrastructure within sixty days.

▶ A VP of Marketing has just seen a competitor lose a key product line due to poor product quality, and immediately ramps up a new marketing campaign to take advantage of this opportunity.

▶ A VP of Sales performs on plan for the first quarter, but sees the second quarter tank and needs something immediately to stem the weak forecast projections for Q3.

These short-term fires happen all the time. Executives rob Peter to pay Paul in the short term to keep the ship (the company and their department) heading in the right direction based on wind gusts, current changes, and the inaccuracies of forecasts.

Talking Trains with an ATL Exec

Back to our formula of:

Goals + Gaps + Options = Quantified Cause

ATL goals are long-term Trains. When there are gaps between the stated goals and what is actually happening, and if they are large enough that some action is required, options are explored. Execs at the ATL level don't want to engage in knee-jerk responses, so the midterm options tend to be changes or additions to current processes to what they had planned to do in the course of that fiscal year.

When calling on an ATL exec, you would ask about goals and options being considered based on gaps in the stated goals for the year. This is simple to explain but sometimes hard to pull off because a salesperson is trained to sell, rather than have the mindset of an investigative reporter, which is what they need.

The second opportunity for a salesperson is the event that has grabbed the attention of the ATL exec because something is changing. It's a classic example of the "If it's not broke, don't fix it, but if it's breaking, get on it!" mentality.

As a salesperson calling on an ATL, you have two avenues to pursue—and you should vigorously pursue both of them.

1.   Ask about goals and options being considered (long term and midterm).

2.   Ask about current events that are causing quick actions (short term).

Now that you have the exec talking, you are taking furious notes, and the opportunity lies right in front of you.

> This is where most salespeople blow it because they believe their job is to come up with answers. This is not their job. Their job is to get the ATL exec to go from the first "I get it" to the second "I get it." They need to cover both Value Conditions.

Now is the time for you to:

1.   Summarize what the ATL has said about their goals and gap, their options, and the short-term events currently in play.

2.   Ask the ATL exec what the best outcome would be.

3.   If possible, tell/show the ATL exec how you can contribute to the best outcome outlined by the ATL exec.

It's as simple as one-two-three. You can call it visioning, vision casting, or strategic planning if you like, but ATL needs to see where they are at now, where they need to be, and then find the things, products, and services that can get them from A to B.

Once again, the ATL exec needs to make this journey on her own. She needs to define the new outcome, possibly with your guidance, but not with your product pitch. Once she envisions the new outcome, she knows she needs to do something different. Her journey from A to B sets the stage for the journey from the first "I get it" to the second "I get it." Your discussion on how you can help them get to the new outcome is their transfer of ownership.

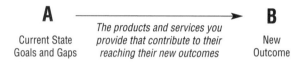

A ⟶ **B**

The products and services you
Current State | *provide that contribute to their* | New
Goals and Gaps | *reaching their new outcomes* | Outcome

BTL AND ATL "I GET IT" TO "I GET IT"

Let's review. The BTL buyer goes from the first "I get it" to the second "I get it" by identifying needs and then either seeing them in operation or getting a chance to work with what you are selling. They are single-focused and need to complete the task.

The ATL buyer is on either one of two journeys.

1. *Journey 1*—He has new goals and is looking at options to implement throughout the year based on plans or gaps that have caused them to want to change what they are doing now to a new outcome.

2. *Journey 2*—An event has caused her to take action. The fire drill has now become a top priority for her, and she needs to take action or the fire will burn out of control.

In either case, you must let ATL execs identify their new outcome (Solution Box B) and then discuss with them how you can help them reach the new outcome.

In the long term, goals and objectives change every year; options need to be formulated and approved. Gaps will be monitored and options modified.

In the short term, it's about being in the right place, at the right time, with the right questions.

So ask yourself, how much ATL training have you had in your career, and how much BTL training have you had? BTL selling is fun, it's competitive, and it's rewarding, with commissions paid out to the winners.

Selling ATL taps into different energy sources, gets you to where the motivation for the change is, and that will get you where you want to be . . . in a great position to get a value decision. Your goal is to get the ATL to see how you can help them get to their new outcomes and contribute to their Trains, even before the BTL buyer presents your proposed solution.

VALIDATION VS. EDUCATION

Stage 3 is a unique stage, and easy to skip over if you are the salesperson. Buyers are doing buyer things, and you must pay attention and stay in control, since both the ATL and BTL buyer are involved, and have different goals.

Education and Validation BTL

The BTL buyer in Stage 3 has accomplished some of his goals already. He has been able to locate at least one vendor with a possibly workable solution. In Stage 2, he did a deep dive into the features and scope of the proposed solution, and it looked like it meets most of the needs. Also in Stage 2, the vendor was looking from their perspective to make sure that what they are selling truly meets the requirements of the BTL.

In Stage 3, the BTL buyer want to make sure what the vendor says they can do, they really can do. In this stage, the BTL buyer's goals are to:

▶ See what they are buying in operation.

▶ Evaluate what they are seeing and relate to how they would use it in their day-to-day job.

▶ Identify any limitations and workarounds.

▶ Ensure completeness of fit.

The bottom line questions are, "Will what they are looking at do the job? Will it accomplish the goals identified so the BTL can obtain the promises made to the ATL exec? Will it work, and not create additional unforeseen problems? Will the user really like it? Is it better than what she has now?"

Education and Validation ATL

The ATL is looking at three things during this stage.

1.   Will it satisfy the BTL buyer, since she is the one who will use it?

2.   Can we get a return on this investment we are making?

3.   Are there any other current or future Trains I can use this asset on?

The first item is pretty easy. To put it in terms of the printer story in Chapter 11, does the printer print to the agreed specification, and is the BTL buyer happy? The degree of the ATL's involvement in this varies, but usually the higher you go, the less involved they want to be, unless it's a pet project of theirs.

The second one, the ROI, is pretty easy as well. The ATL knows the size of the problem, the Solution Box B, the Train, and they can figure out what this will mean to them pretty fast. They can see the gap they have, and can estimate how much of the gap this purchase will fill.

The third item is the real goal for the ATL exec and the salesperson. Can the ATL exec walk away from this stage feeling confident that the following questions can be addressed?

1.   Will this move the chains on my Solution Box B I have identified this solution will address?

2.   Can this move the chains on any other Trains that I have?

3.   Are there other Trains in the company that this might contribute to?

For BTL buyers to go from the first "I get it" to the second "I get it," they need to feel comfortable that what they are buying will fit into their day-to-day routine, will make their job easier, and will meet the identified needs. They are the ones who will be responsible for the implementation of the solution, and they will need to test-drive the car or try on the shoes.

The ATL exec at this stage has different goals. He wants to make sure this solution can make financial difference on his currently identified Trains, and if it can also affect other current or near-term Trains. If it does, then they *really* "get it," and additional value is created.

Back in Chapter 10, we talked about Solution Boxes and the purchasing of a CAD system. If you were going to be in the Stage 3 demonstration, you would see probably three or four engineers and a VP of Engineering. Remember, the VP has a different reason to be there than the engineers. The engineers are making sure that what they are buying will work for them—it's easy to use, there is support when required, and it fits within their budget.

The ATL buyer is there to make sure that what he is looking at will get two Trains out of the station: (1) make a dent in the engineering team's goals of cutting design time by 10 percent over the next two years and (2) lower the cost of product lifecycle engineering by $25M over the next three years.

Imagine that the demo is over, and the team is back in the conference room doing a final review.

SCENARIO #1

At the end of the day, the team adjourns into the conference room, and the salesperson takes center stage. "Thank you all for coming. Let's review what we have seen today." He then goes through a few slides, reviews what they have done that day, explains the final outcome, and asks for questions.

The salesperson feels she has done a good job; the engineers are nodding their heads, and all looks good. The VP says it seems like it was a good day. She feels that the team got what they needed.

SCENARIO #2

The salesperson takes center stage, thanks everyone for their time, then turns to the VP of Engineering and hands her a magic marker. "Could you please do us a favor?" the salesperson asks. "Could you go to the whiteboard and outline what you folks have seen today and what outcomes you saw being impacted?"

The VP takes the marker, goes to the board, and starts writing what the engineers tell her. After a while, the VP is writing a lot more than what the engineers are telling her. "Hey, if this works out, imagine what we could do on Project 11AC. You could cut design in that by 20 to 30 percent if you do half of what we saw here today." She is thinking about other Trains as well.

Obviously, Scenario 1 is the BTL "I get it," and Scenario 2 is the ATL "I get it." So the question on the table is how many Stage 3 sales calls have you had where you were happy with the BTL "I get it" and really didn't go after the ATL "I get it"—in other words, when you settled for the Scenario 1 ATL head nod as validation? Now you know what a mistake that was, and are starting to see how you can change your approach. The ATL and BTL second "I get it" is there for the taking. You just have to ask the right questions.

CHAPTER **16**

Balancing Between the Lines to Accelerate the Deal

Thought we were finished with Stage 3? No way! Stage 3 is complicated. As you learned in the previous chapter, you need to make sure both buyers validate their needs—not once, but twice. Each has separate needs, and you have to satisfy both. You need to win at both the ATL level and the BTL level to get a sale.

It's at this stage that a few things can make or break the sale. They mostly revolve around energy.

ENERGY SOURCES

In Stage 2 and Stage 3, you confirm with the prospect that the company needs to do something different. The ATL buyer is motivated to change what he is currently doing, since what he is doing now is not getting him the results he needs. The BTL buyer needs to change, since the ATL buyer is telling her she has to, so she has come up with her decision criteria list to make sure the product or service they are going to acquire can do the job, and that they can use it efficiently and effectively.

BTL Solution Box: Energy-Light on Change, Energy-Heavy on Selection

The BTL buyer has a direct say on the solution being provided. She is providing the energy for the selection. The overall need to change is not in her sphere of influence, but once the decision to change is made, she certainly does have energy to make a vendor selection.

The ATL buyer has little say in which product or service the BTL buyer wants to buy, except of course when it affects multiple Trains. Then the BTL buyer needs to play nice with the other BTL buyers (Train conductors) to make sure everyone is somewhat happy, and the ATL buyer needs to make sure everyone's agenda and needs are addressed.

ATL Solution Box: Energy-Heavy on Change, Energy-Light on Selection

There is a need for the company to change what it is doing. The ATL exec has had an ATL event and has now stated in quantifiable goals the need to change.

The need to change from what the company is doing is high, but the ATL exec's input on what is actually chosen is low, since he typically lets the User Buyer choose.

The energy source in the ATL world is high, and typically outpowers a BTL energy source. It is what is causing this entire change, evaluation, and purchase to be launched. You need to tap into this energy to make it through the evaluation. It's not just identifying this energy in Stage 2 that's important. It's quantifying and using the energy throughout the evaluation that will give you enough energy to push this deal over the finish line.

Figure 16–1 depicts the different focuses of the ATL and BTL buyer. What's high priority for one is low priority for the other. These are the needs and priorities you must balance.

Energy Gaps

In both the BTL world and the ATL world, there are energy gaps. These gaps are causing the change that makes the prospect look at new or dif-

Figure 16–1 Dueling Priorities

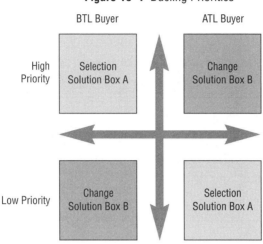

ferent ways of doing what they need to do, and why they are looking to buy what you are selling.

Getting the Job Done BTL

In the BTL world, things are changing. The BTL buyer knows this, but may have no approved budget. The ATL will approve budget for the BTL when:

▶ The new product or service will result in a better ROI over current methods.

▶ In the wake of a change, reorganization, new product launch, etc., the new product or service will contribute to the desired change.

If the BTL has approved budget for a purchase, the energy source will be the BTL feature-and-benefits battle. It will be a competitive slugfest, with the following exceptions:

1. If the BTL key buyer is responsible for other departments/ users/projects that are outside the BTL buyer's scope, then all parties involved must either individually or by committee evaluate the respective viewpoints of each of the participating departments/users/projects. (Not only a mouthful, but a tedious and potentially contentious process.) An example would be a Marketing Manager who is in charge of a

project that crosses sales and customer support teams. The product or service must meet the requirements or both user groups, as well as Marketing's needs.

2. The ATL is convinced that there are other Trains that should be considered. As we've learned, multiple Trains create a powerful energy source.

THE NEW USE OF BUDGET

IBM's BANT (Budget, Authority, Need, Timeframe) is no longer valid. Budget is the wrong qualifying question. You need to stop asking about budget. If whatever you are selling can move the chains on a Solution Box B Train, the ATL will find the money. If you are asking about budget, you are staying at the BTL energy level only and missing opportunities—and big bucks.

MOVING THE CHAINS ATL

The ATL exec usually holds all the cards at the beginning of the sale. The energy levels during a sale are illustrated in Figure 16–2.

Figure 16–2 The Energy of a Sale

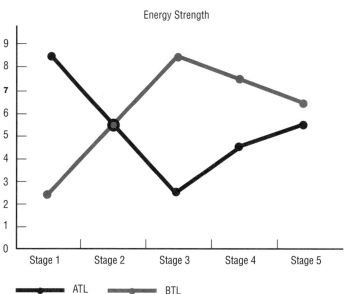

Look at the energy progression of the ATL. It's very high in the beginning, of course. The change that is happening is at the ATL level. The BTL buyer is being kept up to date somewhat, but the change itself is taking place at the ATL level.

At Stage 2, Educate, the change has been quantified, and the ATL is turning over the evaluation to the BTL, since he is the one who is going to have to use whatever is being bought. This is where The Split happens, and both the BTL User Buyer and the ATL exec have equal interest and energy. The BTL is anxious to see what is out there and try all the new toys. The ATL is looking for help on multiple Trains, and now is the time she can create leverage if she needs to with decisions that are being made right now.

By Stage 3, Evaluation, there is some interest from the ATL, especially if the deal affects more than one Train, but usually by this time, the ATL exec has turned things over to the BTL buyer, who is running the evaluation.

Stage 4 witnesses the reappearance of the ATL, as the conversation shifts to money, investment, and ROI, as it relates to time and risks as well.

By Stage 5, the ATL and the BTL involvements are almost equal; if so, the nod goes to the ATL execs, since they are the ones who have multiple trains in the game.

A salesperson should be trying to harness as much energy as possible when it is available, which means that if the salesperson wants to get ATL energy, he has to call earlier than he is probably used to. After all, he was taught to engage the ATL exec near the end of the process.

If you aren't ProActively trying to get ATL energy by the end of Stage 2, you've probably missed the opportunity, and your evaluation will be based on BTL energy only. It's going to be a commodity sale now, and you're probably looking at a discounted deal.

LEARN TO QUANTIFY ENERGY

You now know where the energy sources are, and when they are at their highest. The next step in the process is to quantify the energy. When you quantify the energy on both sides of the line, you will accelerate the deal time frame, since both the ATL and the BTL buyers see the advantage and there really is no reason to wait.

Have you ever been involved in a sale where the ATL and the BTL see the need early, like at Stage 2, and the energy is so great that a deal is done at record-breaking speed? Jill was involved in one such deal.

FORGE VALVE

Many years ago, Jill was selling engineering ERP software and got a lead from a company called Forge Value. The VP of Engineering and the Director of Manufacturing were going to look at buying a system and getting it installed by the end of the year, which was in about five months.

Jill had an initial meeting that went very well, and had just finished a demonstration of the product a week earlier. This sale was looking to be worth around $500K. Jill's quota at the time was $750K, so this was very important for her.

A typical deal of this size would take three to six months. There was a lot of work that had to be done; competitive benchmark demonstrations, high-level negotiations, and system configurations to be finalized.

About six weeks into the sale process, she had a meeting at the Forge factory scheduled for 1:00 P.M. The purpose of the meeting was to prepare for a custom demonstration and get all the details of what Forge wanted to accomplish.

The meeting started at 1:00, and about ten minutes into the meeting, the president of the firm stuck his head in the door.

"Don, have you bought that computer system yet?"

"Just working on it", said Don, the VP of Engineering.

"Stop messing around and buy the thing, today!" said the president, and Jill walked out of there two hours later with an order for $500K.

The energy was large for Forge because they were negotiating on a contract worth $3M and had come to find out they needed the new system in order to get it. Oh, and Don didn't have a formal budget. Jill got the order anyway

---

We should all be as lucky as Jill!

Quantifying BTL is usually pretty easy. Quantified Problems are usually features and functions. It needs to go forty revolutions per second. It has to accommodate fifty users. It has to hold up to 500 pounds. These are easy numbers to get, since the BTL buyer develops them.

The BTL buyer gets involved with ATL-type numbers a little bit, and when they do, it usually revolves around:

▶ *Budget*—an assigned budget dollar amount assigned to the project or the acquisition.

▶ *Time*—time saved on a previous method, process, or task.

An approved budget is usually the quantified Solution Box A for the BTL buyer, and usually it's not enough to make a complete purchase. Rarely does the BLT buyer's budget cover all that he wants to buy.

Time savings are always a good thing. They can be quantified, and the ATL exec, always wanting to do more in less time, will listen and, if the potential savings are substantiated, will allocate funds for something that will save time.

The ATL buyer's Solution Box B is also pretty easy to get—just ask. ATL buyers always talk in numbers, and getting numbers out of them usually requires just asking questions. Getting past the subjective and getting to the objective is a skill, and one that should be mastered to get to numbers.

"You mentioned you would have a revenue shortfall for the second half of the year. How big will it be?"

"Pretty substantial."

Most salespeople would stop here. You now know better: You need to continue and get actual numbers.

"Could you quantify that?"

"Yes. We see a 5 to 6 percent gap between revenue estimates and what we initially forecasted. The difference will be hard to make up, but we need to do it."

Again, most salespeople stop with the vague characterization. Don't settle for responses like:

"It's a key initiative."

"It's very important."

"It's a top priority."

"It is on the top of things to get done as soon as possible." (Doubly vague!)

"It's something we have to get done right away."

These nonquantified statements need to be quantified. Since ATL execs live in a quantified world, getting numbers should not be too hard. Salespeople need to dampen their enthusiasm when they hear words like *huge*, *big*, *very*, *key*, and the like. You have to get numbers to quantify the energy.

If necessary, you can prod for quantification with approximate numbers.

"On a scale of one to ten..."

"How confident are you? Sixty percent? Seventy percent? What number would you apply to this?"

"On a scale of one to a hundred, where would this fall as a matter of importance to get done this year?"

"Would you consider this to be a top-three item for you this year?"

You could also use an Impact Analysis to get some numbers from the prospect.

GETTING TO QUANTIFICATION WITH IMPACT ANALYSIS

How you get quantified numbers from an ATL exec is always interesting. Sometimes they are quite forthright. At other times, you have to develop a strong relationship and mutual trust. Usually it's somewhere in between.

There are times when the ATL exec either just doesn't have a good feel for the numbers, or will not disclose any numbers, or there are so many options that she just can't put a specific number on the desired impact of what you are offering.

If that happens, there is a tool, Impact Analysis, that may help you get some range of numbers from the prospect so they can at least see some sort of quantification of the investment they are making.

The "range of numbers" approach has always been a good way to estimate progress. An economic impact analysis typically estimates the change or progress in goals or activities between two scenarios, one a snapshot of where the organization is today, and one a snapshot into the future, assuming a change has been made. This tool was developed to measure outcome by quantifying the impact of the change that is being looked at.

Companies are no longer buying products or solutions; they are buying a better outcome. And you must be selling a product or service that creates a better business and financial outcome than earlier approaches to solving their problem or meeting their challenge. When companies fail to identify both the strengths and the worth of a project, it becomes more difficult to achieve success. For a project to be successful, you need both commitment from the buying and selling organizations and metrics (numbers) to measure the change (see Figure 16–3).

An Impact Analysis provides the opportunity for buyer and prospect to work together to identify and quantify the business and financial impact of the outcome being evaluated. If an organization believes it lacks the need for the desired outcome or their management does not commit to making this effort successful, the potential results will not be realized.

This assessment is a way for you to get a measured commitment from the buyer early in the process and not only the change they are making, but how you can impact that change as well.

Additionally, it can be used as a homework assignment to qualify or disqualify a selling situation.

Figure 16–3 Probability of Success

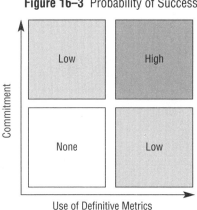

Figure 16–4 Impact Analysis

	Virtual Learning Impact Analysis	
Start 1–10	Rank your abilities on a scale from 1–10 on each of the seven items below, and then total the scores. Start is your starting score. Finish is your score with the new program/service in place	Finish 1–10
_____	Increased market share with insights/planning	_____
_____	Having the right information available	_____
_____	Lowered risk on key decisions	_____
_____	Getting things done faster	_____
_____	Increased project visibility throughout organization	_____
_____	Get beyond day-to-day tasks	_____
_____	Use technology to capture lost revenue	_____
_____ A	Totals	_____ B
	Percentage Difference (B/A) _____%	

Figure 16–4 offers a sample Impact Analysis you could use to get numbers—Quantified Causes, Quantified Problems—from your prospect. Since you are the one driving the sales process, this is a great way for you to insert energy into a deal. It may even be your potential solution.

By performing an Impact Analysis like Virtual Learning's (and substituting items that would be applicable to your industry or products), you can help get some quantified numbers associated with your product or service early in the process. This will serve you well.

Rules for conducting an Impact Analysis include the following:

▶ *Use terms familiar to the prospect.* The topics they are evaluating should be familiar—not buzz words, jargon, or sales-centric words around your features and benefits.

▶ *This is a homework assignment.* You want the prospect to get involved. Doing this over the phone without them seeing it is really not a good idea. The more you get them involved, the more the numbers and the results will be theirs. Get them to do some of the work.

▶ *Get it back fast.* If you do send it to them to complete, make sure you get it back within a few hours, a day at the latest. If you don't put a sense of urgency around this, it will lose energy and significance.

▶ *You can have one analysis for the company, or for the deal, or one for each individual project (BTL) and Train (ATL).* You can combine an ATL and a BTL on one document—or not. Every situation is different, and you must use your judgment.

▶ *Make it realistic.* This is not a document that is supposed to show off your products and services in the best light. Its purpose is to capture the outcomes of what the prospect is trying to achieve. The more realistic you make it, the more the prospect will value you and the Impact Analysis document.

▶ *Put some importance around it.* Do not treat this as a simple exercise. Treat it with some significance, since their outcomes of what they are trying to achieve are very important to them.

There are many ways for you to create energy during a sales process. The energy you capture from the ATL exec, the BTL buyer, and yourself early in the sale will carry you through the process and lessen the chance the deal will tank.

SOLUTION BOXES AND I-DATES

Energy can be found with I-Dates tied into Solution Box A and B. Both the ATL and BTL buyers have deadlines. For the BTL buyer, they have a project or schedule they need to get started on or a committed company deadline. These deadlines also involve others, so when you start looking for I-Dates, look also to see if others are impacted or if there are other critical events that tie into the I-Date for Solution Box A.

For Solution Box B, or ATL Trains, the ATL executive usually has made departmental, intradepartmental, or company commitments that will speed up a decision. These commitments are usually on a schedule, so they will have an I-Date attached to them. Use these I-Dates to:

▶   *Create energy*—Tie what you are selling into these dates.

▶   *Accommodate BBB*—Buyers buy backward, so start with their I-Date and build a timeline backward, making sure all associated I-Dates are taken into consideration.

▶   *Increase energy*—The ATL exec has to meet approaching deadlines and commitments, often ones that the BTL buyer is unaware of. They don't want a delay, since any movement of the committed dates would increase their risk and cause them more time headaches, and possibly impact other Trains in the organization. To avoid this, they will increase their energy at the end of a purchase (e.g., not require a major discount, walk a deal through legal, personally champion other ATL approvals if necessary)—all to have this Train leave the station on time. (More on deadlines in the next chapter.)

With all the material in Chapters 15 and 16, you are now prepared to look at Stages 4 and 5, the proposal and closing the deal.

CHAPTER 17

Stages 4 and 5:
Getting a Decision

The goal is now in sight—the end of the sales process and, hopefully, if you have stayed in control, a positive outcome for you.

A lot can go right or wrong in Stages 4 and 5, but based on all the work you have done so far, you should feel in control. Hopefully both the BTL and ATL buyers have taken ownership of your solution, and you have a better than fifty-fifty shot at this decision. But the truth is, the deal is yours to lose, and you can lose it, if you don't pay attention.

There are ways you can stay in control at every step in the process and get feedback from the customer about whether they are serious (or not—which is just as important to know, and to know early) about going forward with you and your solutions.

THE GOAL IS A DECISION

Business management gurus might define a goal as "a desired result a person or a company envisions, plans, and commits to achieve, usually within a finite timeframe."

If you put this into a selling context, this might be the definition:

> A goal is the end point of a vision that, through sustained effort and small achievements, creates a desired result, within a defined timeframe.

So what happens in Stages 4 and 5 is not the "close of a deal." What you are shooting for is a decision, either yes or no. Let's make the goal here not to close the deal (that would be a push), but to get a decision (that would be a pull), since our definition of close is framed around the prospect's decision, rather than you getting the order.

To close is to get a decision, either yes or no, without delay.

There is a major decision to be made. You need to break down the major decision into several little decisions.

Major Decision

The major decision you are looking for is a yes or no to what you are proposing. Asking for a decision turns out to be so much easier than asking for the order. Asking for the order is so much about us rather than about what the prospect wants to do.

"So Bob, when we are done here, you're going to give us an order, right?" (NOT!)

It's fine to ask that, but it is kind of one-sided. It's all about what we want and really isn't mutual. You job therefore is not to get the order; your job is to do what the customer wants, and that's to come to a decision without delay.

"So Bob, when we are done here, you should be in a perfect position to make a decision by tomorrow at the latest, yes?"

Buyers, both ATL and BTL, want to make decisions. It's what they want to do, so the goal is to get a decision about your solution, either yes or no, without delay (remember Chapter 13's Law of 2X here as well).

Little Decisions

Big decisions are made up of little decisions. It's important to get a decision—a little decision—at every stage in the sales process, since you can stay in control of the process and uncover objections when they arise.

Think of the sales process as a bunch of small decisions the buyer has to make to be in a position to make the big decision. If you ask for a decision every step of the way, this should take the fear out of the prospect making the big decision and help you stay in control of the process. These little decisions also let you continue to qualify (occasionally to *disqualify*) the prospect throughout the entire process.

There are many things you can do in these little decisions through the sales process. Which tools to use, and where to use them, depends on each individual sale.

Transfer of Ownership

Getting a decision at every stage helps the transfer of ownership. It will allow both sides to stay involved and mutually move the decision forward.

"Bob, this has been great. It seems like a next step would be for us to spend some time finalizing what you really want to do here. Are you in a position to make a decision at our next meeting, say Friday at 10:00?"

This is going to throw Bob for a loop, since Bob is usually just dragged from one meeting to the next. He now has been asked to have some skin in the game.

"What do you mean 'decision'? What do I have to decide on?"

"Well, you need to get some information together, and we may require some of John and Mary's time to get the whole picture. You okay with this?"

Having the prospect make a decision at every step ensures that each stage is being considered, and that there is mutual effort involved in getting to the decision.

It's about control, and most good salespeople are control freaks. They can't help it. They have to control their own company's time and resources, their own time, and the prospect's decision-making effort as best they can.

Deadlines Increase Energy

Deadlines have a way of increasing the energy of a deal. And creating deadlines that are *customer*-facing, not sales-facing, is a great way to insert energy into a deal.

A sales-facing deadline might be an end-of-the-month deal, a this-week-only special, a holiday sale, and or an end-of-the-year special.

Customer-facing deadlines might involve the start of their project, other deadlines they face, or deadlines you can impose based on commitments they have made.

A CUSTOMER-FACING DEADLINE

Bill used to run a conference company called Invitational Computer Conferences. These one-day events would have between thirty and forty exhibitors, who would pay him $2,000 to $3,000 for each show to get leads. The conference company would send out 5,000 invitations, about 500 attendees would show, and the exhibitor's local salespeople could meet local prospects. It really was a good idea.

But as you know, nothing is as simple as it sounds. The invitations had to be mailed at least thirty days before the show to make sure the attendees had enough time to put it on their schedules, but Bob had a hard time getting companies to commit to his invitation deadlines.

Companies wanted a discount if they decided to exhibit after the invitations had gone to print and had been mailed out. Their logic was that since their name wasn't on the invitation along with all the other companies, they shouldn't have to pay full price. Marketing departments were usually in charge of the budgets for these shows, and not having their name on the invitation wasn't really a big deal, but it was a negotiating point for them.

It didn't take Bill long to figure out that marketing departments don't care a lot about having their name appear, but they care a lot about their brand and logo. He started printing the invitations with the exhibiting companies' logos on the back flap, in color.

Most marketing departments didn't want to miss a chance to have their logo displayed to 5,000 potential buyers. The "print deadline" became the "logo deadline," and not only did it speed the decisions, it eliminated the discount problem as well.

Use customer-facing deadlines that are important to your prospect to create energy, especially near the end of the deal.

THE POWER OF OPTIONS

The power of options becomes important as you near the end of a sale. People like having options; they like choice. It makes them feel in control; they get to choose the right thing, their perception of a best fit.

People are more likely to purchase when they have more options. It's human nature to purchase an amount *relative to what is available.* When they have a choice of two things, when they have to say yes/no, either/or, one or the other, there is a feeling of deficiency, not of choice. So give your buyers choice, but not too much choice. Read on.

The Power of Three

George Miller at Princeton wrote about short-term memory and the power of numbers (his "The Magical Number Seven, Plus or Minus Two" is one of the most highly cited papers in the world of psychology), but it seems that three is kind of a magical number too, as in:

- Good, better, best
- Bronze, silver, gold
- Small, medium, large
- Red, yellow, green

The list goes on. Three options seem to be the favorite from a negotiations point of view as well. One option is bad, since there will be a winner and a loser. Two is always a break-even at best. With three options, a good negotiator has a lot of room to play with and can give two away, keep one, and still wind up with a win-win.

Storytelling

Telling stories or providing analogies is always a great transfer of ownership vehicle. A good analogy is something that is familiar and easy to understand; it is short, clear, and visual. It is used to enhance a point being made, or to make a comparison so that the message is clear.

Using an analogy at the end of the first few minutes of dialogue is a good idea. It can also be a good way to sum up a current discussion and lead into the next segment.

GETTING A DECISION—NOW

Moving through stages is a good thing, but there are times when an ATL buyer gets cold feet. At Stage 4 or 5, either they feel the pressure of the decision, they have some concerns about how it all works, or they are just having a bad day—for some reason they just freeze. They delay, look for other options, call in additional help, or just don't answer the phone. When this happens, you can turn to a couple of reliable tools: the Cliff-Dive and the Short-Term Transfer.

The CliffDive

Remember, you are selling something prospects do not want to do, like to do, or have done for them. You are asking a prospect to do something they hate doing.

You are asking them to *change*, and people and companies hate to change. It's why the ATL buyer may flinch near the end.

People are always comfortable with the way they are doing things now, even though they know they have to change to stay ahead. If they are forced to change, they probably do not understand all the consequences, so they may be getting a bit nervous or a bit overwhelmed.

They are not getting back to you because they don't want to implement this change, invest in your idea, or even buy your product. Because actually, they do, they really do. It just seems like it's such a big investment, such a big step forward, such a huge risk . . . They feel it's like . . . jumping off a cliff.

Well, jump off the cliff with them, with the CliffDive. But use this tool with the ATL buyer only. It's a tool to use when you are near the end of the sale, when you think the prospect is getting cold feet. They are not returning your calls, and when you do talk to them, they are evasive and noncommittal.

"We still have some final things we have to go over."

"There are still a few more people we need to get buy-in from."

"Really, we'll be ready to go ahead next week."

You have heard them all before. This deal is going to fizzle out, and you need to do something quick.

Use the CliffDive to take some of those irrational fears and put them into perspective. Fears are what really drive decisions—to either completion or delay (remember the AWAY questions from Chapter 5?). Even the fear of not making a decision is a powerful motivator. But lucky for you, fear is in the mind. Oh, it's real, but it is in the mind, and you can use that fact to help the prospect overcome their fears.

The CliffDive stretches out the fears and risks the prospect sees right now. You know exactly what the prospect is going through with your proposal. They have come to a point in time and have to make a decision. The prospect is nervous because they have stalled. It's as though this process they have been involved in has now come to a head, and a decision has to be made . . . *the* Decision.

It better be the *right* decision. It better be great, profitable, and one that all the BTL people can use. It also has to be able to be implemented, measured, and useful for all the Trains that have been identified.

With that much pressure on the decision, you wouldn't want to make one either.

What you need to do is to stop the prospect from looking at the decision as a point in time, as one step in time.

Start where the prospect is today and take him through time in two steps.

Step One is to start from *today* and take him to *tomorrow* (typically thirty to sixty days out). Ask the prospect this question: If they implemented your solution, started using the item purchased from you, or put into operation the product/service you are offering, and it really was doing well . . . how would they feel?

Today ————————————————▶ Tomorrow

FEEL?

"Pretty darn great."

"Very relieved."

"It would be terrific."

The prospect says these small sentences, these few words describing feelings, which create a mental picture that captures a moment in time—but a time that is different than *today*, and one that moves the prospect away from all those fears they have about making a decision.

Now the prospect has one set of feelings about where they are *today*—fear-based feelings—but now he also has the feelings of *tomorrow*, which are great feelings. The more the prospect thinks about the tomorrow feelings, the less the fears of *today* will rear their ugly head.

You don't want to stop now. You have moved the prospect to the edge of the cliff—so far, so good. Now have him jump off the cliff. Have them do a CliffDive, right to a time slot, about three to six months out, that is called NEXT, and NEXT is a really great place.

NEXT is where the prospect desperately wants to be. At this point, you lead your prospect to say all the great things he will be doing when the decision that is being pondered right now is finally made and is behind him.

NEXT is a great place. It's a place the prospect wants to get to. Now your solution is seen as just one step in the process, rather than that big cliff you want them to jump off.

CliffDive lowers their fears and minimizes risk. The decision is just a step in the direction they want to go, not a giant leap, like they are thinking it is right now.

Why did I specify that the CliffDive is only for ATL decision makers? Because only decision makers know what is next; only decision makers have the vision and the strategy in place to see what's next. BTL buyers are waiting to be told what to do, so when you ask them what's next, they really can't tell you because they haven't been told yet.

But use this tool at the decision maker's desk, and the results will be a shorter sales cycle. Additionally, the desire of the prospect to "get a good deal" has been minimized as well, since it is now just one step in the master plan, you are moving the chains, and therefore it's a first step they need to take.

The CliffDive is a tool to use to get the ATL exec off the dime, put their fears to rest, and help them through the process of change. Prospects want and need to change. They just need a little help in jumping off that cliff.

Short-Term Transfer of Ownership

Short-Term Transfer of Ownership is a tool to use if either the ATL or the BTL buyer gets stuck with completing their buying decision (see Figure 17-1.) It helps them accept transfer of ownership and take a small step right after their decision.

The I-Date, the date they are going to start using the solution you are providing, is a great tool to talk about when the buyer is going to start implementing what you have sold them. What about right after the decision? Time-Traveling them to the point right after they make their decision may release the decision roadblock.

Figure 17-1 Short-Term Transfer of Ownership

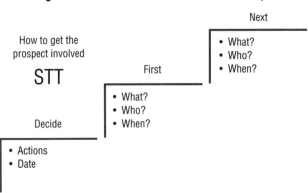

I bought a used sports car a few months ago. The choice was between two cars, and I was really interested in my wife's opinion, since she would be riding in it as well from time to time—and besides, it's *always* good to ask your wife's opinion.

It was down to a silver one and a yellow one, and since I have really only had black cars, the yellow one was getting my attention.

I told my wife that I was going to buy the car the next day, which relieved her, since we had been looking for a long time. I also told her that I had made a decision, and I thought the yellow car would be a great choice.

"That's great," she said. "But if you expect me to get out of a yellow car next week at that formal party, you're probably mistaken."

Yep, silver car it was (and it was a great choice). My wife's Time-Traveling me to a week after the purchase made the decision so much clearer.

What are your prospects doing in the short term—the first ten days—after their decision? Usually, they have no idea how they are going to get started. Oh, you've told them what you are going to do to help them be successful, but they have no clue what to do first. Have a meeting? Okay, so they'll have a launch meeting, but what will they do second, third, and even fourth, in those early days to make sure they get this investment off to a good start?

If they can't tell you, give them some hints, best practices, suggestions. Make it real for them. It has to become their idea. They have to put some sweat equity into the process.

Thinking what to do first should take the pressure off the *decision* and get them back to thinking about the *process* (good), not the *event* (bad). If they cannot think about the process, the deal is in trouble because with no transfer of ownership, there's no urgency, no energy—and quite possibly, no deal.

Making a decision is hard. If you keep the momentum going in a forward, positive motion, you have helped the buyer take some "little baby steps" toward a solution they really want.

CHAPTER 18

How to Implement ATL/BTL Selling in Your Current Process

I'm not out to change the world, your life, or your selling style. I do want to give you more chances to call higher in a prospect organization, and have meaningful conversations that will help you and the prospect, both ATL and BTL, make informed decisions.

Above the line and below the line thinking should not be hard to integrate into your current sales process. The biggest move is to manage by stage and manage expectations for both buyer and seller by stage. What do you want to do and get, stage by stage?

MAP YOUR STAGES

The first thing you need to do is map your stages. Somewhere between four and six stages would be great. If your sales process is pretty simple, four should be okay. If it's a very complex sales process, still, no more than six stages. The vast majority of you should settle at about five stages, as we have discussed in Chapter 2.

These stages should mimic your buyer's buy process. You should have an idea of what you want to have happen in each stage:

▶ By stage: for the ATL exec; the BTL buyer; the sales team.

▶ By activity: homework assignments; Gives/Gets; key qualification and disqualification questions.

▶ By decision points: at each stage; options at the end of the sales process.

Overlay Tools into the Process

Once you have mapped out the process, socialize it (have some other people look at it), and make sure it's as complete as possible. Test-drive it on a few deals that are currently in the funnel to make sure you have captured what needs to be applied.

Your mapping-out process need not be all-inclusive, since trying to cover every nuance would be very hard to administer. The goal of this process is to allow the salesperson to tackle ATL and BTL issues separately and understand that each one needs something different than the standard sales pitch.

BUILD STAGES INTO YOUR CRM SYSTEM

The ability to track activities by stage in your CRM is very useful, and taking it to the next step, tracking the number of days spent in each stage, will be eye-opening.

In most cases, you'll see a 20 to 30 percent drop in the total length of your typical sales cycle, not immediately, but over time. This will happen because you'll find yourself focusing on best-practice number of days by stage. Do you remember our Better Sales Timeline from Chapter 11? It's worth repeating here:

Better Sales Timeline

Stage 1	Stage 2	Stage 3	Stage 4	Stage 5	
3	7	5	3	2	Days total: 20

It's amazing how much more efficient sales teams can become when they see how much time they waste.

VISUAL COLLABORATION WITH THE CUSTOMER

Over 65 percent of people learn best visually, so the fact that salespeople send emails and text messages without any visual anchor or reminder is baffling.

Gap Charts, Journey Maps, and Short-Term Transfer and Impact Analysis tools exist to help you have a more visual impact with both your ATL and BTL prospects.

Gap Charts

The Gap Chart is a tool you need to master as soon as you can. You can start using it on the first or second call you have with an ATL exec.

The key to using a Gap Chart successfully is practice. You need to do it a few times to get good at it, so practice it—on your boss, senior execs of your company, and even ATL execs from your current customers.

Stay away from using you or your company name during the development of a Gap Chart. The more you talk about how you can solve or what you can do, the less time you will be spending in front of the prospect talking about their favorite subject, which is them, of course.

A Gap Chart like the one shown in Figure 18–1 can be used to guide you through a conversation with an ATL exec and will lead to a quantified cause. You don't want to sound like a marketing brochure, so make sure

Figure 18–1 Sample Gap Chart

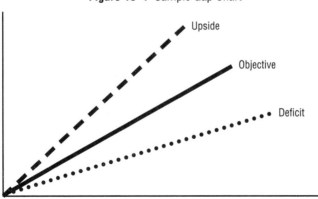

you've done your homework and can speak about their executive persona (see Chapter 8)—and that you've learned enough about their company so you can ask intelligent questions:

> *"So Mr. Smith, you have identified a key GAP in your 2015 plans. As you strive to close this deficit gap, what do you see as your risks?"*

> *"So, Ms. Jones, looking at your goals for this year, and the upside GAP potential, what are the things you are doing to try to close that gap?"*

The more you practice, the better the results and the transfer of ownership from the executive will be.

Journey Maps

The more templates you have of Journey Maps (Chapter 13), the better. Share them around the office. Make it a common practice to work through a Journey Map when you are reviewing a sales process with your boss.

Post the Journey Maps on your wall, so they remind you of the sales processes you're involved in and so others can see your work and take away some best-practice ideas. And share your best Journey Maps not just with sales management, but also with marketing management. Let marketing see what is happening with these tools, and they might be able to put a different spin on the whole thing.

As noted earlier, always make sure your customer is working with you on this effort. Many deals have been lost because Journey Maps were done by the salesperson with no input from the ATL or BTL prospect.

A sales process is a living thing, with new twists and turns all the time. This reality should be reflected in your Journey Maps. Keep them updated, moving, and extended—sort of like a rolling thirty- to sixty-day project. By Stage 4, the Journey Map will include the contract sign date and the I-Date and maybe even items developed in discussions of the Short-Term Transfer ten-day window.

You'll find that the ATL part gets ahead of the BTL part and vice versa, and that's normal; they're traveling at different rates, on different paths.

One goal of the Journey Map is to allow for more control for both you *and* the prospect—and no control for the competition. Another is to add value for both parties and to help the buyer reach a decision, either yes or no, in a timely manner.

NEXT-STEP SELLING

All great sales calls start with the end in mind. You *never* go into a sales call asking yourself, "What do we want to say? What do we want the prospect to hear?"

You go into a sales call with the attitude, "If all goes well, this is the next step we should take, and by this date."

It's all about control and pulling the buyer through the process, at every sales touch and sales call. It's about thinking what is the next step, what does the end of the call look like in your mind, what action steps should be assigned?

Before you start a call with the prospect, especially an ATL exec, you want to plan for your final summary.

Three Parts to a Sales Call: Get the Order Right

You have a call next Wednesday, and it's an important one. You want to be prepared. How should you prepare? Here are the three elements of a good sales call:

▶ *The Intro*—How you kick off the sales call, that first minute or two that sets the stage.

▶ *The Middle*—The content of the sales call, what you are planning to talk about, the agenda for the meeting.

▶ *The End*—How you wrap it up and control the next step in the process.

All great sales calls start with the end in mind, so you start with the last element first. Before you even think about the intro or the middle, you must know the answers to the following questions:

"If this call goes well, what is the next step I want to have happen?"

"What is the best outcome for all parties, and what is our next step?"

"What does each of us need to do when this meeting is over?" (The vital homework assignment!)

Yes, this sounds a little backward, but if you don't have a goal, a direction you want this call to go and where to end up, you will end up directionless, which of course is not good, since then someone other than you can take control of this sale, which would be bad.

> In a directionless sales call you can have a great meeting and discuss a bunch of topics, but at the end, no one knows where to go from there. Participants start throwing out options until enough people agree on something—anything!—and *voila*, action points are announced and a follow-up meeting is scheduled. Not good! Especially not good for the salesperson.

Every sales call needs a leader, and a leader knows up front what they want the outcome to be. And hey, other options may come up that would be even better than the one you planned for. Great! Spontaneity is good—and it's all the more reason you need a structure to plan for the end of the call, as well as the ability to modify the end if something unexpected happens during the meeting.

Build a Sales Call Backward

Since you know the steps of the buying process, you should usually be aiming for the next step in the buy process. If you are at Educate, pull to Validate; if you're at Validate, move to Justify; and so on.

To start with the end in mind, you have to really plan for it, really think about it. There is so much going on, especially when you are going to be doing a presentation, a demonstration, or trying to qualify a prospect. You are so busy trying to accomplish the task at hand, you can forget that you are on a journey.

Build the sales call backward. Ask yourself, really ask yourself,

"If this call goes well, what is the next step for each of us—me, the ATL, and the BTL?"

Once you have those outcomes in mind, then you can build the outline of what you want to have happen on the call. Start with the next step first. What's the goal, the direction you want the call to take? . . . then start the call. Since buyers buy backward (see Chapter 14), you may want to build your sales call the same way.

Summarize, Bridge, and Pull

Probably one of the easiest tools to use in a sale is the Summarize, Bridge, and Pull (Figure 18–2)—"SBP" for short. It's what you need to do at the end of every sales call to stay in control, but you need to plan for it at the start of the call.

Figure 18–2 Summarize, Bridge, and Pull

Summarize   Bridge   Pull

An SBP is how you end every call, meanwhile addressing your goal of determining whether you want to continue down a sales process with the prospect. Every call has to end with an SBP. Every call. It's the only way to maintain control in the process. First, here's an example of an SBP.

"Well Mr. Thomas, we seem to have covered quite a bit today. You said you want to: one, decrease your costs by getting your products through the manufacturing process 10 percent faster than is happening today; two, lower the time it takes to create custom orders; and three, avoid sales discounting on most of your deals (three for them)*.*

We also discussed how my company might be able to contribute to some of these areas (one for us)*. Would you agree we have had a productive meeting?"*

"I agree; we've had a good meeting."

"Great. It seems to me that the next step would be to sit down and learn more about each other: what you want to accomplish, and how we can help you. Then, you'll be able to determine if we should go any further. Does that sound okay?"

An SBP has three parts. They are:

1. You/I
2. The bridge
3. The next step

You/I

This is where you summarize the discussion you just had, making sure you put the prospect's position first. Never put "I" first. Start with an introduction statement, then go right for a "You" statement and follow the 3:1 rule.

THE 3:1 RULE

Three things for them for every one thing for you. Remember, it's all about them.

The Bridge

Here is where the salesperson prepares the prospect to go across the bridge with him. This is not losing control, since you are the one proposing the bridge. Ask the prospect if they are ready to go across the bridge.

THE BRIDGE

"Would you agree we have had a productive meeting?"

"I agree. We've had a good meeting."

Usually the buyer agrees, since it is a summation of the conversation that just took place. You want them to agree that they had a good meeting—but are not looking for agreement on the issues you discussed. They are agreeing that they said this, you said that, and it seems worth exploring.

In some cases they may not agree, and you will uncover a hidden objection that may have to be dealt with. It is better to uncover an objection early in the sale than to let it drag on to the end and be the one thing that stalls or kills a deal.

Next Step

This is when you propose the next step in the sales process. The "next step" functions as the "Pull" in our SBP.

NEXT STEP

"Great. It seems to me that the next step would be to sit down and learn more about each other: what you want to accomplish, and how we can help you. Then, you'll be able to determine if we should go any further. Does that sound okay?"

In most cases, the prospect agrees since it is a natural next step in the process. You have completed an SBP and are in control of this sales call and this deal. Figure 18–2 offers a visual summary of the process.

An SBP must be done after every meeting, after every conversation. It is very easy to lose control of a deal. It can happen in a split second, usually at the end of a meeting when a prospect takes over and sends the deal in a different direction than you want it to go.

When the client proposes a next step, a salesperson might think one of two things:

1. Well, they're the ones buying. If we do what they tell us to do, we should get the order.

2. Okay, I'll let them dictate the next step, but after this step I'll gain control back.

Neither of these thoughts is good for the sales process. You're in a battle for control. Don't let the client tell you what to do, since it would make you reactive rather than in control. An SBP is a tool to be used at the end of every sales call to keep control every step of the way.

Salespeople who practice each step of the SBP before the sale starts are the ones who will stay in control of the process. Own the process, own the deal.

Summarize, Bridge, and Pull is a powerful tool in the salesperson's bag. You'll get to a point where you will feel strange if you do not use an SBP in a meeting. That will be a good sign, since without an SBP, control of the sales process is up for grabs. Use it to stay in control of every meeting and every sale.

The overall goal of implementing SBP into your sales process is both strategic and tactical. Stage management, days in stage, and roadmaps are strategic. It's how you roll it out and measure success that is really going to prove this out in the long term.

The tactical tools—like the Journey Map, SBP, and Gap Charts—are ones you need to practice daily. Be intentional in your use of them. Practice a lot.

Focus on one tool or tactic at a time until it becomes second nature. When you do this, you will be able to incorporate your changes on a tactical basis week by week.

Whatever you do, you need to start somewhere. That first step is usually the hardest, since you are doing what you are asking the ATL exec to do—change. You don't like change either, but selling the way you are doing now is not the answer.

CHAPTER **19**

Overall Strategizing for an Above the Line Sale

If you have read this far, you see the advantage for calling high earlier in a sale. Salespeople all over the globe agree the trick isn't calling high. The trick is knowing what to say when you are there, knowing what to say that will be of value and that will let you *stay* high.

Hopefully, this book has given you answers and some insight into the world of calling at the ATL level, and why it's different than calling at the BTL level. You need to win at both levels, as we have said, but why on earth would you bring the same messaging to the ATL exec as you do the BTL buyer? The printer story should always remind you that a Quantified Cause is a different value proposition than a Quantified Problem.

This of course asks the big question: Why are salespeople trained only on Quantified Problems? That's a great question. Rarely will you find a company training the sales department on executive personas, Trains, and gaps. Nor will you find sales managers asking sales reps for this information. No matter how green or how experienced the sales manager, you will hear:

▶ Who is the prospect?

▶ What are we selling them?

▶ Is it budgeted (Solution Box A)?

▶ Who is the decision maker?

▶ When are they going to close?

▶ Who is the competition?

It looks like the sales world has Box A pretty much covered, which leaves Box B for you.

Here are some final tips for your quest to be better in the sales world, and to shorten those sales cycles and stop the need for last-minute deals and steep discounts.

MANAGING RISK BY RELYING ON NUMBERS

If you want to take one thing away from this book, it's numbers. ATL execs will rarely do anything unless there are some numbers, any numbers, to make a decision. In most cases, it will be the size of Solution Box B, the value of the Trains, the size of the gap, or the value in the Value-Star. In some cases, these numbers can be developed or created through good questioning skills or with Impact Analysis tools.

Numbers justify the risk involved in the change the buyer has to make. I just heard a story about a bicycle shop owner who did not have control of his numbers. A few years ago, he did not order enough inventory, so he believed he had left money on the table. He could have had a bigger year if he had ordered more.

Not wanting to make the same mistake twice, he doubled his order the next year, again, not taking the time to really understand his numbers. Of course, the economy went south, and he went bankrupt. He closed his doors after fourteen years in business. What caused him to double his order? Greed? Experience? A gut feeling?

When faced with change, ATL execs are going to make some decisions; it's what they do. The less they can rely on gut feelings, and the more they can quantify their decisions, the less risk they are going to have to deal with, and you can help them by working out the numbers with them.

Numbers also prove to the ATL that they are working to make an impact on their Trains, which is what they get paid to do. They have to show to their bosses that they are making progress on their commitments, and that progress is always expressed in quantified terms.

This *Is* a Big Deal

Working with numbers is not optional. Selling ATL and BTL are two different sales, two different languages (the kid's table and the adult table), and therefore, if you don't catch it early—before The Split—you will have a tough time catching up.

Separation—when you are at Stage 4 with the buyer and the ATL is way back at Stage 1 or Stage 2—is unfortunately pretty common. Salespeople believe the BTL when they say they have a need, it's been budgeted, and they are the decision maker. Well, it's true, they have a need, it has been budgeted, and—from a User Buyer's perspective—they are the decision maker.

But if you believe this too strongly, you will ignore the second value proposition, equal in importance to the first value proposition. This is the value proposition that directly addresses what is causing the change; it speaks to the motivation behind the product or service being bought. Find the answer to these questions:

▶ What is causing the ATL to change what he is doing?

▶ What are the results the exec expects?

▶ What are the timing and risks associated with the change?

▶ What if he doesn't change right now? What will happen and what will be lost?

The second value proposition is all about the strength of that change.

Measure a Sale's Energy and Use It

The motivation behind change is energy, and energy can be measured. You have seen through Gap Charts, Impact Analysis, and questioning via the ValueStar that you can measure the energy of a deal, since you should be able to quantify Solution Box B and find a number of Solution Box B's Trains to help the prospect justify making a favorable decision about what you are selling.

Way too often salespeople let the energy of the BTL buyer guide their decisions for presentations, demonstrations, and the final negotiated price. That's not to say that the BTL buyer doesn't have energy and an agreed budget for making a decision. It is to say the decision will be made more quickly—and usually with a higher sales price—if you tap into the energy that exists above the line.

KNOW YOUR OPTIONS

If decisions were black and white, then sales would be a pure numbers game. The problem is that buyers rarely want to be pinned down with an either/or decision. People like choices, and the probability of a decision in your favor is greater if you are the one providing the opportunity to choose.

Research has shown that people don't like too much choice. An overabundance of choice results in confusion and sometimes even depression, since if there too many choices, a perfect one cannot be made. When confronted with too many choices, people start to consider trade-offs. When these trade-offs are being considered, a salesperson needs to be working with the ATL buyer.

Yet people are happy when they can "logically" make a good choice. ATL and BTL buyers want to be involved and explore their options. They want to feel good about their choice. Options and choice are good. Sending a one-choice proposal at the end of Stage 4 to a prospect seems a bit silly, doesn't it?

Vague vs. Concrete

The emotional satisfaction salespeople get when a customer expresses vague enthusiasm is illusory. *Soon, better, a lot, a ton, key, ASAP,* and the *top of the list* are all great words to hear, but they are not quantifiable.

For BTL buyers, the pressure of quantifying is limited by their needs. They want the features and benefits of what they buy to give them certain things. They can give you feeds, speeds, and specifications to meet all day long.

Since they have been given a budget, their ROI needs are really non-existent, and this is where the subjective nature of their decisions creeps in.

You have to get numbers, concrete numbers, when you are working on a large deal. These numbers include:

1. Size of the company, both in revenue and number of employees

2. Size of Solution Box B and Trains

3. Gap numbers in performance initiatives

4. The amount the chains will be moved with your solution

5. The overall amount the solutions or Trains will be worth to the company

That's it. It's not a big list, nor is it a complicated set of numbers. No higher math and fancy equations. And if you are helping the ATL buyer determine these numbers, then you are gaining a competitive advantage and influencing the decision in your favor and at your asking price, since the value of the Trains you are helping is far greater than the amount of money you are asking for your product or service.

For the deals that are going to get most of your attention—the whales, the important ones, the ones that are going to make or break the quarter or year—you need to get numbers and get them early. The troubling part of this is that for most salespeople deal management is about what they are selling, rather than about what the customer is buying and why.

"For every store they are opening, the prospect is spending $1.5M on store location data and analysis. With our solution, they feel they can cut this to below $1.0M per store and save 20 percent of the time that it takes to look at all alternatives. With ten store openings scheduled in the next twelve months, they feel we can help contribute to over $5.0M in savings and at least two months of effort."

This example is from a salesperson who has obviously been talking a lot to the ATL execs and exploring options. It's about how to close the gap between what it takes to open a store (in terms of investment of both dollars and time) and what the C-suite wants or needs that investment to be. The changes the prospect is willing to invest in to make this happen is what is really key here.

How many conversations like this are you having? Get to Quantified Cause early and you will increase your chance for success.

Numbers from Them

A general rule is that numbers must come from the customer. You can help by showing examples of ROIs and testimonials from other companies that claim a typical 10 percent increase or a 25 percent decrease after they bought your product. This information is a good validation for the ATL exec, but in a true transfer of ownership mentality, numbers must come from them. If they don't take ownership of the numbers, they won't take ownership of your solution, ATL or BTL.

Time-Traveling is a way to make numbers real. You should never live in only two dimensions when talking to ATL execs. They live their entire business day in the last few months or the next few months. You need to include ". . . over the next few months" or ". . . over the past few months" in every question you ask.

Influencing speed and velocity takes place on a high level. To use another football analogy (yes, I confess, I love football), when a quarterback goes from JV football to varsity, one of the biggest differences is the speed of the game—it's so much faster. The same is true when the quarterback goes from high school to college, and then from college to the pros. The game gets faster. And a quarterback succeeds when the game "slows down" for him. You'll hear it all the time. The more experience the quarterback gets at a certain level, the more the game slows for them.

The same thing can be said about going from BTL to ATL. The timeframe expands, and the speed of change is important. The BTL buyer has a deadline, which is usually a date. It's a single dimension, and really has no time movement in it.

The ATL buyer has Trains coming in and out of the station. The timing of a decision is really important, and that's what they are really thinking about—the things that they can or cannot affect. Your head is going to be spinning, and things are going to seem to proceed so much faster when you start hanging out at the ATL level.

At the ATL level, they are thinking about the last three to six months and the next three to six months. That's what they can impact, so that's where your questions need to be directed.

WINE AGES WELL. PROBLEMS DON'T.

From a sales point of view, the phrase would be "Wine ages well. BTL-driven deals don't."

The ATL buyer has Trains in their station, and they need to get those Trains out, to allow other Trains to enter. The Trains are overdue. The exec needs solutions to get the trains out of the station. They need something; they need to add, delete, or change something to get the Train moving.

Problems don't go away; they need responses—action. That action comes at the ATL level. If there is no change being implemented, it's probably not an important Train.

If you're working on a deal that has low energy—that is, the problem is not really a big problem—then either:

1. Drop the deal, and revisit it another time.

2. Find additional Trains so the energy of the deal and of the ATL exec increases.

LOOK AT ALL THE OPTIONS

So, "Find additional Trains," is it? If only it were as simple as those three words.

Problems in organizations rarely only affect one department. Find Trains that are impacting multiple departments, and you may find more important Trains than the one you are holding on to. However, adding Trains and finding other initiatives is rarely easy, nor is it as clean as a deal that involves a major initiative or a big Train. The larger the deal, the more Trains it involves.

ATL executives have problems that span across:

▶ Projects they are working on

▶ Initiatives that cross departmental boundaries

▶ Revenue shortfalls

▶ Projection of goal targets for products or by customers

▶ Cost issues

Rarely are these company functions attached to one Train. You, as the conductor of the orchestra (to mix the metaphor), are paid to get all these functions together and to identify where what you are selling can impact the Trains that are being addressed.

It's true, it's not easy. If you end up dealing with too many people or too many Trains, you probably need to even go higher in the organization, and when you do, don't forget to:

▶ Time-Travel.

▶ Find gaps.

▶ Ask ValueStar questions.

▶ SBP, starting with the end in mind.

FINAL THOUGHTS

It's the mission of this book to bring to light the gap in selling value to customers. The idea of "selling value" (push) has always fascinated me. Why are we in such a hurry to push our ideas, thoughts, products, and services at the prospect, rather than ask questions and develop the answer *with* the prospect (pull)?

Calling high to the ATL exec is another concept that is fascinating, inasmuch as salespeople know they should do it, but rarely do. The ATL value proposition is different than the BTL value proposition, and every salesperson, sales manager, and marketing executive should take notice. Salespeople will do what is being looked at by their management, but all too often sales managers are not inspecting ATL activity and creating marketing messaging to attract ATL prospects; they are ignoring half the value the prospect is willing to apply to your solution. They are asking you to ride a bicycle with one wheel, play a piano one-handed, or try to walk using only one leg. Hey, you can do that if you want to, but there seems to be an easier way. Now that you've worked your way through the first eighteen chapters, you know what you must do—and I've tried to give you the tools to do it with.

Find Problems or Goals

If the prospect has a goal, if they have obstacles to overcome, if they have a challenge, you can bet they're going to be changing something. They need to close a gap, which would imply the need to expend energy. Find their Trains or Solution Box Bs and quantify them, and you are tapping into an energy source.

The Courage to Stay ATL

It takes courage and commitment to change—whether the change is an ATL exec trying to get something done in her company or your ability and desire to change the way you have always sold (we like to stick with the old success patterns). Like most things, when you try something new, it's scary, and at first you might not do it as well as you will eventually. Practice does make perfect, so keep practicing some of the tools and concepts we have covered in this book.

Work with BTL

Of course, your job is to work with BTL buyers, not ignore them. You probably already have a thousand ways to sell to the BTL buyer, to find needs and develop solutions for their Quantified Problems. Work with them and get the BTL value proposition. It's important, but it's only one wheel on the bike.

Know the Difference

You should be encouraged that you now know the difference between selling above the line and selling below the line. In twenty years of sales and sales management training, I've learned that it is the salesperson and sales team that get both prospects' value propositions out early—what they want to buy (BTL) and why they want to buy it (ATL)—who succeed.

Here's to your success, to your customer's success, and to better tools to help you sell.

Index

Above the Line, *see* ATL... *entries*
action information, 67
American Automobile Association (AAA),
    158
analogies, 204–205
ATL/BTL selling
    implementing, 210–219
    The Split in, 18–20
    time frames in, 225
    see also specific topics and stages
ATL buyers (Fiscal Buyers), 36–48
    ATL numbers from, 140
    BTL buyers in meetings with, 149
    and Cause and Effect Split, 20–21
    concerns of, 19, 20, 22
    education and validation for, 185–187
    encouraging decision making by,
        205–209
    energy of, *see* ATL energy
    fear factor for, 39–41
    goals and initiatives of, 37
    homework for, 79–80
    "I get its" for, 177–179
    and Level 3 purchasing, 35
    motivators for, 41–44, 50
    outcome important to, 12
    personal wins for, 35
    Quantified Cause for, 129–130, 177–178
    Quantified Solution for, 130, 134–135
    resistance to change in, 37–39
    separation of BTL buyers and, 122–123
    talking Trains with, 181–183
    three-dimensional selling to, 47–48
    time dimension for, 42, 44–48
    time frames for, 180–183
    vocabulary of, 136, *see also* ValueStar

ATL energy, 49–60
    capturing, 49–54
    and change, 50
    creating and controlling, 150–160,
        see also controlling the ATL sale
    in Evaluation Stage, 188–192
    and events affecting buyers, 54–57
    quantifying, 192–195
    sources of, 162
    tips for working with, 58–60
ATL Journey Maps, 157
ATL Outcome, 7, 8, 12
    BTL split with, 18–20
    and Customer Buying Process, 9
    satisfying, 11–12
    targeting, 15–18
    in value proposition, 15
    see also individual topics
ATL selling
    BTL split with, 18–20, 29–30
    courage needed for, 228
    energy early in process of, 53
    golden rule of, 152
    overall strategizing for, *see* strategizing
        for ATL selling
    rules for, 78
    training in, 184
    see also ATL/BTL selling; *individual*
        stages of sales process
average order size (AOS), 54
average sales price (ASP), 54, 58
AWAY messaging, 96–97, 152
AWAY questions, 50–51

BANT (IBM), 191
basic need quality, 125–126

being ProActive, *see* Initiation (Stage 1)
belief perseverance, 42
Below the Line, *see* BTL. . . *entries*
Bentham, Jeremy, on pain and pleasure, 49
boiling point events, 54–55
bottom-up viewpoint, 108–109
Brand/Image, in ValueStar, 148–149
brands, 148
bridge phrases, 98–99, 217
BTL buyers (User Buyers), 8
    ATL buyers influenced by, 43
    attitude of, 33–34
    budget for, 54, 128, 194
    and Cause and Effect Split, 20–21
    concerns of, 19, 20, 22
    education and validation for, 184–185
    energy of, 170–171, 188–191
    Five Ps for, 31–33, 125–129, 170–171
    "fix it" mode of, 42
    and Level 3 purchasing, 35
    in meetings with ATL buyers, 149
    needs checklist for, 177
    outcome important to, 12
    ownership taken by, 178
    present focus of, 45
    Quantified Solution for, 130
    reasons for concentrating on, 24–28
    separation of ATL buyers and, 122–123
    Short-Term Transfer of Ownership tool
        for, 208–209
    two-dimensional selling to, 46–47
    vocabulary of, 136, *see also* ValueStar
    "Why wait?" question for, 171–172
    working with, 228
BTL energy, 170–171
    in Evaluation Stage, 188–191
    quantifying, 192–195
BTL Journey Maps, 157
BTL Outcome, 7–8, 35, *see also individual
    topics*
BTL selling, 23–35
    ATL split with, 18–20, 29–30
    and BTL buyers' attitude, 33–34
    definition of, 7
    and Five Ps of WIIFM, 31–33
    and levels of purchases, 34–35
    as only half of the value, 28–29
    personal wins with, 35

rationale for, 24–28
targeting, 15–18
training in, 26, 184
for User Buyers, 11, 12
in value proposition, 15
see also ATL/BTL selling;
        features-and-benefits selling;
        individual stages of sales process
budget, 54, 128, 191, 194
business acumen, 12–14, 108–119
    and ATL/BTL Solution Boxes, 114–118
    and change as motivator, 109–111
    and I-Date for Box B, 118–119
    and thinking across entire organization,
        111–114
    and top-down and bottom-up
        perspectives, 108–109
    and Trains metaphor, 115–119
business case, 6
business risk, 142–143
buyers
    internal and external customers of,
        151–152
    leading, 155
    multiple personalities of, 20–21
    priorities of, 60
    see also ATL buyers; BTL buyers
Buyers Buy Backward (BBB), 173–174, 199
buying for yourself (Level 1), 34

calendar, of ATL buyers, 59–60
cause, 41
    as energy, 72
    Quantified, 129–130, 177–178, 220
    quantifying, 53–54, 56–57
Cause and Effect Split, 20–21
change
    and energy in Evaluation Stage, 189
    fear factor with, 39–41
    forced, 39
    is issue for ATL buyers, 50
    as motivator, 109–111
    motivators for, 41–44
    in priorities, 58–59
    resistance to, 37–39
change events, 55
Chief Executive Officer (CEO), 83, 109
Chief Financial Officer (CFO), 83, 84

Chief Information Officer (CIO), 83
Chief Marketing Officer (CMO), 84
Chief Operations Officer (COO), 83
Chief Revenue Officer (CRO), 84
choice, 204, 223, *see also* decision making;
        options
C-level executive personas, 82–84, *see also*
        ATL buyers
CliffDive tool, 205–208
closing, in traditional process, 16
Closing the Deal (Stage 5), 192, 200–201,
        See also decision making
cold calling, 73
comfort, of ATL buyers, 42
commodity quality, 126
company information, 67, *see also* business
        acumen
company wins, 35
competitiveness, 25–26
conformation bias, 42
control
        of inbound sales, 68–72
        with Journey Maps, 213
        through transfer of ownership, 202
controlling the ATL sale, 161–174
        and BTL energy, 170–171
        by building value across Trains, 163–164
        and Buyers Buy Backward (BBB),
                173–174
        with deadlines, 162–163
        by finding additional Trains, 161–162
        Gap Charts for, 165–170
        and gaps, 164–165
        with I-Dates, 172–173
        with Journey Map reviews, 172
        with special offers, 174
        time adjustments in, 165
        with "Why wait?" questions, 171–172
CSP (Customers Solve Problems) mantra,
        51–52
Customer Buying Process, 8–10
customer-facing deadlines, 203–204
customer referrals, 74
customers
        of buyers, 151–152
        buying cycle of, 10
        numbers from, 140, 225
        point of view of, 5–8

visual collaboration with, 212–214

deadlines, 162–163, 203–204
decision making, 200–209
        in Customer Buying Process, 9
        deadlines for, 203–204
        Five Ps checklist for, 125–129
        in five-stage sales process, 18–19
        little decisions in, 202
        for major decisions, 201
        managers' fears about, 43
        power of options in, 204–205
        risk factors in, 144–146
        shortening time to, 153–154
        in Stages 4 and 5, 200–201
        subjectivity in, 224
        Three Levels of Why in, 63–66
        tools for stimulating, 205–209
        and transfer of ownership, 202
Decision stage, 18, 19
Demonstrate/Validate stage, 18, 19, 175–
        177, *see also* Evaluation (Stage 3)
demonstrations, 8, 9, 16, 18
directing sales calls, questions for, 101
Director of Operations, 83
disqualifying leads, 62, 67, 68
door knocking, 73

ease of use, 32, 127–128
Educate (Stage 2), 18, 19, 120–135
        in energy progression, 192
        and Evaluation Stage, 175–177
        "how" of, *see* controlling the ATL sale
        printer illustration of, 130–135
        Quantified Cause in, 129–130
        Quantified Problem in, 124–129
        Quantified Solution in, 130
        trumpeting in, 158–160
education process, 120, 184–187, *see also*
        Educate (Stage 2)
emails
        in Initiation Stage, 85–89
        of 30-Second Speech, 100
        for trumpeting, 93, 94
emotion, in third level of Why, 66
emotional value, 148–149
energy, 150–160
        cause as, 72

energy *(continued)*
 created by salespeople, 152–160
 early in ATL selling process, 53
 in Evaluation Stage, 188–195
 increased by deadlines, 203–204
 and Lead Energy Matrix, 61, 63
 measuring, 222–223
 quantifying, 192–195, 222–223
 sources of, 152
 see also ATL energy; BTL energy
Evaluation (Stage 3), 175–199
 and ATL buyer concerns, 180–183
 energy sources in, 188–192
 I-Dates in, 198–199
 Impact Analysis in, 195–198
 quantifying energy in, 192–195
 Solution Boxes in, 189, 198–199
 validation vs. education in, 184–187
 Value Conditions in, 176–179, 183–184
events affecting buyers, 54–57, 181
Executive Assistant, 84
Executive Manager, 84
executive personas, 82–84, *see also* ATL
 buyers (Fiscal Buyers)
explicit lead scores, 63
external customers, 151–152

failure, fear of, 40–41
fear, 39–41, 153–154, 206, 207
features-and-benefits selling, 3–6, 20, 24–28,
 see also BTL selling
Fiscal Buyers, see ATL buyers
Five Ps, 31–33, 125–129, 170–171
five-stage sales process, 18, 123–124
framing prospect's problems, 96–97
Freud, Sigmund, on pain and pleasure
 principles, 49
future, ATL buyers' focus on, 44, 46

Gap Charts, 165–170, 212–213
gaps, 164–165, 189, 190
Gives/Gets, 68, 69, 80–81, 174
goals, 201, 228
 of ATL buyers, 37, 164–165, 185, 186
 of BTL buyers, 184–185
 gaps between performance and, 165–170
golden rule of ATL selling, 152
Google+, 74, 76, 77
here to help approach, 69

Hill, Napoleon, 40
homework, 75–77, 79–80, 196, 198

IBM, 191
I-Dates (Implementation Dates), 118–119,
 157
 controlling ATL sale with, 172–173
 in Evaluation Stage, 198–199
 moving, 173
 and Short-Term Transfer of Ownership
 tool, 208–209
"I get it" conditions, 176–179, 183, *see also*
 Evaluation (Stage 3)
image, in ValueStar, 148–149
Impact Analysis, 195–198
implementing ATL/BTL selling, 210–219
 mapping stages in, 210–211
 and next-step selling, 213–219
 visual collaboration with customer in,
 212–214
implicit lead scores, 63
inbound sales, 61–72
 control of, 68–72
 disqualifying leads for, 62, 67, 68
 in Lead Energy Matrix, 61
 lead scoring for, 62–63
 qualifying leads for, 62, 67, 68
 Three Levels of Why for, 63–66
 and trumpeting, 93–94
in-depth (Mama Bear) homework (Level 2),
 76–77
"I need your help" speech (phone messages),
 89–90
Initiation (Stage 1), 82–107
 asking questions in, 100–103
 options at end of, 106–107
 paraphrasing and summarizing in,
 104–105
 phone messages in, 89–92
 prospecting strategy and tactics in, 82–84
 short emails in, 85–89
 30-second speech for phone calls in,
 95–100
 Time-Traveling in, 105–106
 trumpeting in, 93–94
Initiation stages, 18, 19
initiatives, of ATL buyers, 37, 165, 168, 169
internal customers, 151–152
introducing yourself, emails for, 88

Journey Maps, 155–158, 172, 213–214

Law of Prospecting, 100
Law of 2X, 153, 154
Lead Energy Matrix, 61, 63
lead scoring, 62–63
left-field words, 66
levels of purchases, 34–35
leverage, 146–147
LinkedIn, 74
long term (for ATL execs), 180

"The Magical Number Seven, Plus or Minus
    Two" (George Miller), 204
mapping stages, 210–211
marketing materials, 26–27
marketing value of organizations, 6
midterm (for ATL execs), 180–181
Miller, George, 204
mini-homework (for prospects), 79–80
money, 138, 163–164
motivator(s)
    for ATL buyers, 41–44, 50
    change as, 109–111
    pain and pleasure as, 49–51
    prospect's homework as, 79
    and Three Levels of Why, 63–66

needed change, defining and refining, 8
need(s)
    BTL checklist of, 177
    to change, identifying, 8
    validating, *see* validation
need to register approach, 69
network of concerns, 14–15
neuroscience of selling, 2–3
next-step selling, 213–219
nibbling, 69–70
numbers
    from customers, 140, 225
    for evaluating options, 224
    for risk management, 221–223
    as vocabulary, 57
    see also quantification

Office Manager, 84
online social tools, 74
options
    assessing, 226–227

knowing your, 223–225
power of, 204–205
outbound sales, 61, 73–81
    getting past screeners in, 77–78
    Gives/Gets in, 80–81
    homework for prospects in, 79–80
    in Lead Energy Matrix, 61
    levels of homework for, 75–77
    qualifying prospects for, 73–75
    rules for, 78–79
    and trumpeting, 93–94
    see also prospecting
outcomes, 6–10
    ATL, 7–9, 11–13, 15–20
    BTL, 7–8, 35
    different audiences for, 12
    as what companies are buying, 196
ownership
    and decision making, 202
    emotional, 148
    taken by BTL buyers, 178
    through questioning, 101–102
    transfer of, 152, 157, 202, 204–205,
        208–209

pain, 49–51
paraphrasing, 104
past, ATL buyers' focus on, 44, 46
perceived power, 163
perceived quality of fit, 31–32, 125–127
perceived value, 32
permission, purchase with (Level 2), 34
personal wins, 32–33, 35, 128–129
personas, executive, 82–84
phone calls, 30-Second Speech for, 95–100
phone messages, 89–92
pleasure, 49–51
present, BTL buyers' focus on, 45
price to value ratio, 32, 128
priorities, buyers' reassessment of, 58–59
ProActive, being, see Initiation (Stage 1)
problem(s)
    dealing with, 226
    Quantified, 124–129, 177, 220
    in reaching goals, 228
    see also gaps
problem-solving motion, 101
product knowledge, 5–6, *see also*
        features-and-benefits selling

professional support/ease of use, 32, 127–128

Proposal (Stage 4)

   in energy progression, 192

   getting a decision as goal of, 200–201,
      see also decision making

Journey Map in, 213

proposals, 9, 16, 18

Proposal stages, 18, 19

prospecting

   to ATL level, 82–84

   in five-stage sales process, 18

   homework in, 75–77

   Law of, 100

   in traditional sales process, 16

   see also outbound sales

purchases, levels of, 34–35

qualification

   for inbound sales, 62, 67, 68

   for outbound sales, 73–75

   through little decisions, 202

   in traditional sales process, 16

quantification

   of cause, 53–54, 56–57

   of energy, 192–195, 222–223

   with Impact Analysis, 195–198

   of time, 140

   see also numbers

Quantified Cause (QC), 129–130, 177–178,
   220

Quantified Problem (QP), 124–129, 177,
   193, 220

quantified ROI, 140

Quantified Solution (QS), 130, 194

questions

   ATL, 149, *see also* ValueStar

   AWAY and TOWARD, 50–51

   in golden rule of ATL selling, 152

   for identifying Three Levels of Why, 65

   for Initiation Stage, 100–103

   for qualifying/disqualifying leads, 67–68

   in 30-Second Speech, 97–99

   Time-Traveling, 104–106

   "Why wait?", 171–172

quick look-see (Baby Bear) homework
   (Level 1), 75–76

Quid Pro Quo (QPQ) method, 68

"range of numbers" approach, 195–196

rapport building, 70–72

reactive, ATL buyers as, 72

reactive response events, 55

real (Papa Bear) homework (Level 3), 77, 80

referrals, 74, 87–88

regulation quality, 127

rejection, fear of, 153–154

Request for Help phone messages, 89–91

request for information (RFI), 160

return on investment (ROI), 6, 32, 35

   ATL buyer's interest in, 54, 185

   ATL selling as about, 11–12

   quantified, 140

   subjective, 140, 144

   in ValueStar, 137–140

revenue, 163–164

rewards, 3, 27–28

right-hand rule, 46–48

risk

   and CliffDive tool, 206, 207

   using numbers to manage, 221–223

   in ValueStar, 142–146

role-playing, 103

sales boot camp, 26, 27

sales calls

   backward building of, 215–216

   parts of, 214–215

sales cycle, customer's buying cycle vs., 10

sales-facing deadlines, 203

salesperson's energy, 152–160

sales process

   control of, 155

   defined with Journey Maps, 155–158

   five-stage, 18, 123–124

   mapping stages in, 210–211

   selling above and below the line, 18–20,
      see also ATL/BTL selling

   traditional, 16–17

sales reviews, 179

Savage, Adam, on deadlines, 163

screeners, getting past, 77–78

self-focus, 2–3, 6

selling money, 138

separation, 122–123, 222

short term (for ATL execs), 181

Short-Term Transfer tool, 208–209
Smith, Will, on danger and fear, 40
social scoring (of leads), 63
social tools, online, 74
Solution, Quantified, 130, 194
Solution Boxes, 114–119, 189, 194, 198–199, 221
special offers, 69–70, 174
speed, 58, 225
The Split, 18–20
    honoring, 120–124
    occurrence of, 192
    see also ATL/BTL selling; two-part value
        proposition
storytelling, 204–205
strategic vision, 180
strategizing for ATL selling, 220–228
    dealing with problems in, 226
    knowing your options in, 223–225
    looking at options in, 226–227
    using numbers to manage risk in,
        221–223
stress, countering, 72
subjective ROI, 140, 144
subjective words, 57
subject lines (emails), 86–87
Summarize, Bridge, and Pull (SBP) tool,
    216–219
Summarize and Flip (30-Second Speech), 99
summarizing, in Initiation Stage, 104–105

"talk about us" mentality, 27–28, 33
thank-you notes, 74–75
Think and Grow Rich (Napoleon Hill), 40
30-Second Speech, 95–100
three-dimensional selling, 46–48
Three Levels of Why, 63–66, 102
3:1 rule, 217
time
    as energy source, 171
    and Law of 2X, 153–154
    quantifying savings of, 194
    in ValueStar, 140–142
time adjustments, 165
time frames
    in ATL/BTL selling, 225
    for ATL buyers, 180–181
    in decision making, 206–207, 225
timelines, sales, 123–124, 211

time quality, 126–127
Time-Traveling, 42, 44–48, 149
    in Initiation Stage, 105–106
    to make numbers real, 225
    questions focused on, 104
    and ValueStar questions, 141–142
timing events, 55–57
top-down viewpoint, 108–109
top quality, 126
TOWARD questions, 50–51
traditional sales process, 16–17
training, 26, 184
Trains, 115–119, 225, 226
    building value across, 146–147,
        163–164
    company functions attached to, 227
    deadlines for, 162–163
    discussing, with ATL execs, 181–183
    finding additional, 161–162, 226
    midterm options for, 180–181
    revenue producing, 164
    risk issues with, 145, 146
    time issues with, 141
Train Stations, 150
transfer of ownership, 152, 157, 202,
    204–205, 208–209
trials, emails about, 88–89
trumpeting, 93–94, 158–160
Trumpet RFI, 160
trumpet update, 158–159
20-Second Pattern Interrupt Speech, 91–92
two-dimensional selling, 46–48
two-part value proposition, 10, 222
    and business acumen, 12–14
    and company's network of concerns,
        14–15
    focus on, 22
    for full-value focus, 29–30
    and multiple personalities of buyers,
        20–21
    selling (Level 3), 35
    targeting BTL and ATL outcomes for,
        15–18
    and traditional sales process, 16–17
    see also The Split

unknown, fear of, 40
urgency information, 67
User Buyers, *see* BTL buyers

validation, 8, 9
    in Demonstrate/Validate stage, 18, 19,
        175–177
    in Evaluation Stage, 184–187
value
    from ATL and BTL perspectives, 174
    built across projects, 146–147
    built across Trains, 163–164
    creating, 137
    differing meanings of, 144
    emotional, 148–149
    perceived, 32
Value Conditions, 176–179, 183–184
value proposition, 10
    of ATL buyers, 35, 51, 52, 227
    of BTL buyers, 28–29, 52, 227
    dual, 151–152
    and separation, 222
    see also two-part value proposition
ValueStar, 136–149
    brand/image in, 148–149
    leverage in, 146–147
    risk in, 142–146
    ROI in, 137–140
    time in, 140–142
vendor selection, 189

Virtual Learning Impact Analysis, 197
visual collaboration, 212–214
vocabulary
    bridge phrases in, 98–99
    BTL words and ATL words in, 174
    left-field words in, 66
    numbers as, 57
    for speaking to ATL buyers, *see* ValueStar
    subjective words in, 57
voice mail, see phone messages
VP of Engineering, 84
VP of Manufacturing, 84
VP of Operations, 83
VP of Sales, 84

warm calling, 73–74
"Why wait?" questions, 171–172
WIIFM (what's in it for me), 7
    for ATL buyers, 43
    Five Ps of, 31–33, 125–129
    questions shifting attention to, 102
    ranking order for, 129
    30-Second Speech questions about,
        97–99

XING, 74